AF383240

Heart Quantum Leap

Your heart moves the world
How we are connected to everything

Petra Ross

About the book

Everyone has a longing within them to be happy and to make a difference in life. This is inherent in human beings by nature, because they are part of this great creation and represent the crown of what God created. But most people live an isolated life from the great divine system and are no longer aware of their power.

The author uses her life story to inspire readers to experience the power of their own heart, which can literally move the world. She also shows us how we can easily become a helper of good everywhere through the language of our heart and the reception and communication of divine powers. She finds these experiences confirmed by the latest scientific findings in quantum physics, which she explains in a clear and understandable way. The author shows people and the world ways to new quantum leaps.

About the author

Petra Ross has been a state-recognised spa and wellness trainer since 2009. She has run a massage studio for 15 years and teaches relaxation techniques such as Qi Gong, autogenic training and progressive muscle relaxation according to Jacobson. She also utilises divine energies and her knowledge in her work for the benefit of her clients. Together with her husband, she passes on this knowledge in lectures on a voluntary basis.

Heart Quantum Leap

YOUR HEART MOVES THE WORLD

How we are connected to everything

PETRA ROSS

Herz-Quantensprung

5th edition 2024

Imprint

Texts: © Copyright by Petra Ross
Cover: © Copyright by Petra Ross
Updated translation from the German **5th edition 2022**.

E-mail contact via: birgit.knelicht@firemail.de

**Publisher: BoD · Books on Demand GmbH, In de Tarpen 42, 22848 Norderstedt, bod@bod.de
Print: Libri Plureos GmbH, Friedensallee 273, 22763 Hamburg
Covergraphics: Designed by Bedneyimages / Freepik Images,
Book block graphics: Bedneyimages / Freepik, Pixabay,
Pexels, images bythe author.**

ISBN: 978-3-7693-0534-0

Contents

"Belief is not knowledge"
the logic of the mind tells us.
But when we firmly believe in something
have had repeated personal experiences,
we have gone from believing to knowing.

In this book, I share my knowledge with you,
of experiences that have been confirmed for me many times over.
May it inspire you to experience the same.

For we are all children of the Most High,
who can unfold their divine potential.

With love and the very best wishes.

Chapel: Unterhofalm in Filzmoos

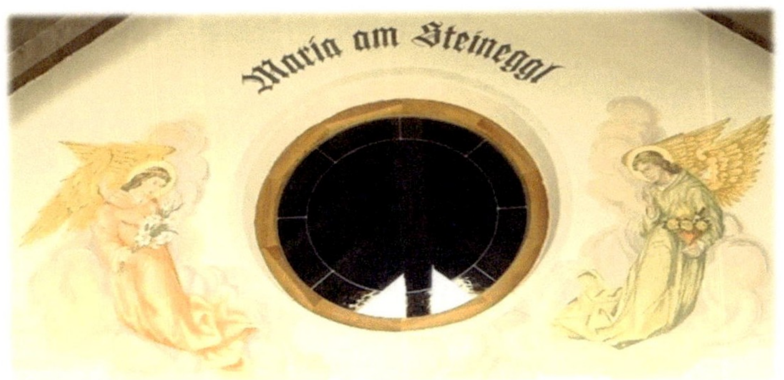

In living nature, nothing happens
that is not connected to the whole.

Johann Wolfgang von Goethe

"There is a universal
energy field
that connects all of creation."

From the lecture: **"In harmony with
the divine matrix"**
by Gregg Braden

Foreword

Sometimes it takes deep crises in life, such as depression, illness and strokes of fate, to create completely new experiences. Experiences that eclipse everything I have experienced so far. From the age of 28 to the present day, triggered by a life crisis, I have had completely new and interesting spiritual experiences that have enriched my life enormously and totally broadened my horizons. I would like to share this with you in order to give you, I hope, completely new impulses for your life.

After being told three times in four weeks by different people that I should write down my experiences in a book, I did so. Because I know that it is life itself that encourages me to pass on what I have been given.

Each of us is something very special, a part of this great universe. We can easily find access to the forces of divine creation that help and heal us. We can use the power of our heart to utilise these energies to help us everywhere. Because everything in this world reacts to the language of our feelings, which comes from the heart. It acts like a programming code on matter and can change it.

I have explained this fact in a chapter using scientific approaches in an easily understandable way to show you that these are natural laws. On an emotional level, we can connect to everything in creation like a child and make them our friends and helpers, even thank them and be a small transmitter of good in the world ourselves.

With this knowledge, everyone has an incredibly great potential to bring about and attract visibly positive things in their own life, in their environment and everywhere on this earth. However, in my book I also make it clear how negative thoughts and feelings have a destructive effect on the sender and everything else.

All my experiences have made me realise this: We are only a tiny part of this universe, but we have a very powerful effect on the overall system through the way we think and feel.

I would like to describe this on the basis of my experiences so that you too will feel like being a conscious part of this creation (to go deeper into this matter). Because the time is ripe for everyone to make completely new experiences, to live our true creative abilities from the heart and to have a healing effect on the big picture.

Chapter 1
The drama: Fallen out of paradise
- Cry to heaven for help -

My twin sister and I were born into a farming family in 1961 as the 3rd and 4th children. We were not planned by our parents and so there was a lot of work to do in addition to working the farm and fields. Thank goodness we still had our grandmother on our father's side to help look after us. A lot of it revolved around farm work, we children were provided with food and clothing, but there was hardly any time for loving care. I say that without blaming my parents, they were very conscientious and passed on their experiences to us one-to-one.

My sister and I were very anxious as children. As our parents and grandma were busy with chores around the house and farm, we often ran after them to avoid being alone. This made us unfree and we couldn't develop any real trust in them or in life. In order to compensate for the depressive moods and anxieties that were already emerging at that time, we developed a rocking mechanism on the sofa until we were eleven years old to calm ourselves down inside. The frequent nosebleeds, my soul's cry for love, ended with the veins in my nose being sclerosed. But that didn't change the underlying problem. We learnt to compensate for our lack of attention with hard work and achievement, because that's how we received the attention and recognition we so longed for.

So we had already fallen out of paradise, being loved only under certain conditions. I felt unfree and dependent on people and duties, because I believed I always had to achieve something special. My life felt heavy. This pattern of performance continued through school, training and work and increasingly sapped my strength. I was heading towards burnout without realising it. I didn't find the love and recognition I wanted in partnerships either. It always ended in a dead end of dependencies and unfulfilled expectations from one side or the other. At the age of 24, during a period of unemployment and after the breakdown of a relationship, I fell into a deep depression with many physical complaints, loss of appetite and insomnia. That was a very bad phase of my life.

Life itself also frightened me, sometimes it seemed scary. Why did the neighbour die so young? Why did the accident happen? Why did the aeroplane crash, the bus crash? Why did environmental pollution and natural disasters happen? Are there laws according to which all this happens? Did we cause it, can we take countermeasures? What is the meaning of life? How can I become happy? I had long harboured a deep desire to be able to help other people, but I really lacked any basis for this.

At the age of 27, after several breakdowns, a six-week cure helped me. Shortly afterwards, I was again suffering from a great lack of strength and constant inner restlessness, as if my core was searching for something it had not yet found. Depressive moods, sleep disorders and frequent back pain were my constant companions. I was desperate because I couldn't go on like this. My father calmed me down in the morning when I sat in front of him feeling weak and sad and didn't know how I was going to get through the working day. He comforted me with words like: "When you think you can't go on, a little light will come from somewhere. Petra, we have Jesus." To which I replied, depressed: "Where is Jesus, why isn't he helping me?" One evening I sat on the edge of my bed, desperate and exhausted, and prayed to God that he would show me a way to get out of this crisis. It was more of a desperate cry for help than a prayer.

Chapter 2
Heaven responds,
immersed in a world of love and light

A month later, I was walking through Herford city centre after work and came across an information stand. The picture of a man I didn't know with the text: "There is no such thing as incurable, God is the greatest doctor" attracted me. I went to the stand and heard about a healing power that came from God and that several people had received healing even today. I learnt that the man in the picture was called Bruno Gröning and had already died. It was credibly described that he had the knowledge of where the illness came from and how it could be eliminated. That the illness was something bad that came via the soul (bad thoughts) and could therefore only be cured via the soul (faith, absorption of the healing power).

I stood in front of the stand with my arms crossed and listened to the conversations. A helper approached me and advised me: "Spread your arms and hands apart, otherwise you won't be able to feel the "Heilstrom" / healing current." He told me that he had been cured of angina pectoris and chronic sinusitis and that his mother had prayed for him. A young man expressed sensitively and very patiently that he had become free of depression through Bruno Gröning's teachings. One gentleman told me with absolute credibility that he had been healed of chronic stomach ulcers from which he had suffered for 20 years. During the talks, I was very touched on the one hand, but also very sceptical on the other. For a moment I thought: "Can this be true? Surely they're not crazy people!"

The fact that Mr Gröning was a Catholic Christian who called on people to follow the teachings of Christ gave me confidence. So I gave them my address. On the way to the car park, I stopped several times in front of a shop window and cried, I was so moved by the encounter. My interest was so great that I went to an information lecture. The then director, Grete Häusler, of the non-profit organisation Kreis für natürliche Lebenshilfe e. V., internally Bruno Gröning Freundeskreis (hereinafter referred to as the Circle) welcomed me and the other guests very warmly. There were several cured people present, as well as contemporary witnesses from back then. All those interested were kindly asked to put their illnesses, worries and everything that was going wrong in life in the past, to give it up in order to be able to receive the new, the good, the healing. We were encouraged to observe what was going on in our bodies during the lecture. I was sceptical, but also excited and interested in what was to come.

Mrs Häusler gave a detailed and very lively account of the three healings she had received during a lecture by Bruno Gröning in Gräfelfing in 1950. The good words she spoke literally filled the room, spreading a loving and confidence-inspiring vibration that did me a lot of good. At the end of her talk, she said to those of us seeking help: "If you also want to get well, then ask God to help you, because man is too weak on his own. But if you ask Him, then also believe what the proverb says: evil is powerful, but God is almighty. And if you believe that and take on a new faith in the good, that God is the greatest physician, then this healing power will begin to flow through your body." At that moment, I felt as if something spiritually heavy had fallen away from me, I almost fell off my chair. Afterwards I felt very light and experienced a pleasant flow of energy in my feet. Other people then gave very impressive accounts of their help and healings and two contemporary witnesses also described their experiences from back then.

It all sounded and felt so new and yet my soul felt at home, a recollection of what had once been. The existence of a spiritual world from which I had long been cut off in my consciousness and to which I had now regained access and a connection. At the end of the event, everyone present was asked what they had felt. I felt light and liberated and was touched by the good wishes for us all. I left the lecture theatre as a different person and was completely changed.

When I got home, my sister immediately noticed the positive change in me. She asked me what I had done, I looked so happy. I enthusiastically told her what I had experienced and she was very impressed. In the evening I received confirmation that something really wonderful had happened to me during this one lecture. I was able to fall asleep and sleep through the night immediately and permanently, which had not been possible for four years. I also felt much more strength and motivation to do something again. From deep inside I was so happy, I felt liberated and felt so much love, the all-forgiving, divine, unconditional love that can help and heal. It's a feeling as if your heart is taking wings. There are no words for it, you just have to experience it for yourself.

Colleagues at work and friends also noticed my positive change: "What's wrong with Petra, she doesn't look so tight-lipped any more" or "You don't have any dark circles under your eyes any more. What have you done? You look completely different."

I was and am infinitely grateful to the Lord God that He answered my prayer. But much more had happened for me, I experienced something like a tangible reconnection with God, the religio. A feeling of having been born again, of only now really living. I had never had such a deeply moving experience before. I was able to realise: "I am not dependent on people at all, but only on God." Until then, my life had largely consisted of performing in order to gain recognition. In the lecture, I was given healing from the highest level without me having to do anything. I realised that this would be a turning point in my life. But of course I asked myself how it was possible that I could now sleep again. After all, I had only sat and listened to the lecture for four hours. I wasn't given any medication, therapies or anything else. Is it possible to become healthy through a spoken word, through the love of the speaker, through the healing power that I had absorbed with open hands? It's all spiritual, even though the body is physical. I was able to experience that healing is possible in this way.

Many interesting experiences followed over the next few years, which I would like to tell you about. But I also had the inner urge to scrutinise the new path more closely. According to the motto "Test everything and keep what is good", I wanted to get to the bottom of this matter and put it through its paces. I thought to myself that if something wasn't right here, I would find the problem.

I will tell you about this in the next chapter.

The first steps on the spiritual path
with loving guidance.

Chapter 3
Convince yourself,
the first steps on the spiritual path

Although I had such a wonderful experience and many more followed, I was still sceptical. My mind kicked in and wanted answers to my questions. Why ask Bruno Gröning as a transformer for the divine power, the healing current / "Heilstrom"? After all, we have Jesus, who redeemed us through his death on the cross! Do his statements agree with the teachings of Christ? Surely this is not a sect!

All these questions were not answered in my mind, but were gradually understood in my heart through experiences and coincidences.

At the beginning I read valuable books that Grete Häusler had written about Bruno Gröning: "Here is the truth about Bruno Gröning", "Experiencing salvation, that is the truth", "I live so that humanity will be able to live on". These books really appealed to me. Furthermore, his original lectures, recorded on tape, are very instructive. He urges us to follow the teachings of Christ and talks about what we must do in order to experience salvation. Gröning said of himself: *"I wouldn't have had to come if people had followed the teachings of Christ"*. In the years after the war and right up to the present day, there was still much that was in need of redemption and repentance.

The following incident helped me to get answers to my questions: A Christian person, whom I told about this healing method, doubted Bruno Gröning's work. He himself had called on people at the time: *"Give me your illnesses and your worries! You can't deal with them alone. I'll carry them for you."* The lady thought that was impossible. She said that only Jesus could heal because he was the Saviour. I should renounce the matter. She strongly advised me to read the Gospel of John in the Bible, then everything would become clear to me. I did so and was strengthened in my conviction.

Jesus was also not yet established at the time and people wondered who he was to perform such miracles. Is he the Son of God or is he casting out devils with Beelzebub? Back then, people also had to convince themselves. Recognising a tree by its fruit is still the best yardstick. And the fruits of Bruno Gröning's work back then and today are incomparably good. From my understanding, he has brought the events of 2,000 years ago back to life for us today. My heart rejoiced at this profound realisation.

From time to time, people need visible helpers and signs so that faith in the divine and salvation can be reawakened in them. The mother of Jesus, Mary, is also a called one who passes on the requests for help and healing. The many plaques of thanksgiving at the chapels and places of pilgrimage bear impressive witness to the fact that the prayers have been answered.

The apparitions of the Mother of God, for example in Medugorje (Bosnia-Herzegovina)[1], Fatima (Portugal), San Sebastián de Garabandal (Spain)[2], Guadalupe (Mexico)[3] also bear witness to God's love, his desire to redeem and help. I read the book "The Children of Fatima" *and* it made a deep impression on me. The Mother of God appeared to the three children Jacinta, Francesco and Lucia, asking them to pray and make sacrifices on behalf of the people, as otherwise the country would suffer greatly. They accepted the mission in childlike earnestness and prayed fervently every day, wore penitential belts, starved and sacrificed many resulting misunderstandings. Jacinta and Francesco were taken to heaven as a sacrifice of atonement for the Portuguese people while they were still children. This spared the Portuguese people a great deal of suffering.

---

1 I saw the Mother of God: book by Janko Bubalo and Vicka Ivanković
2 Garabandal - The index finger of God, 1 January 1993, by Albrecht Weber
3 The Miracle of Guadalupe, Lars Fischinger - Book - 20 million pilgrims a year

What particularly touched me in the book was the statement by the Mother of God, Mary, that the heavenly Father was very sad that people acted and lived as if he had not sent his Son Jesus Christ to earth for our salvation.

And yet, out of his unconditional love for us humans, he once again sends or calls chosen people who can consciously bear suffering and karma vicariously. The Fatima event, the sacrificial life of the stigmatised saint and expiatory soul Therese Neumann from Konnersreuth[4] and the life of the stigmatised saint Padre Pio[5] clearly bear witness to this. The Italian Padre Pio bled daily for from his five stigmata every day for 50 years. According to him, they hurt as much as if there were nails in the stigmata that were being turned. During his holy masses, he mentally experienced the agony of the crucifixion, which he offered up for the salvation of mankind. A great deal of help and healing came about through his intercessions and suffering. Bruno Gröning's path of suffering[6] also bears witness to his willingness to help those in need. He expressed this with the words: *"I have already walked my way of the cross."* The same applies to the many other stigmatised people around the world who remember the suffering of Christ and voluntarily carry out karma and make sacrifices for other people in seclusion with a joyful heart.

Everywhere on earth, God finds ways to help people. In India, for example, there are masters who instruct their students in divine things in ashrams. If a master deems it necessary, he carries out something on his own body on behalf of the disciple in order to help him and help him progress spiritually faster. The yogi Paramahansa

---

4 The life and death of Therese Neumann von Konnersreuth
5 Padre Pio: His life, love and suffering
6 Revolution in medicine, Chapter 7, The unrecognised suffering, Dr
  Matthias Kamp, MD

Yogananda reports in his autobiography in the chapter "Our Journey to Kashmir" on page 263 about his teacher Sri Yukteswar, who voluntarily took a life-threatening illness but recovered. Sri Yukteswar had burnt many sins of his disciples through his fever in order to help them. Highly developed yogis can direct other people's illnesses to their own bodies. Just as a strong man can help a weaker man carry a heavy burden, a spiritual master can alleviate the physical and mental suffering of his disciples by taking on some of their karma.

Baird Spalding's book "The Lives and Teachings of the Masters in the Far East" also bears witness to the impressive abilities of these personalities and also to their love and willingness to make sacrifices to help other people.

God's love for us is infinite. He also recognises that humanity is usually no longer able to overcome the suffering it has caused itself. That is why he has created the possibility for his children to pass on their own guilt, their own karma, to another by inwardly detaching themselves from it. In his book, the physician Dr Matthias Kamp explains that a person called by the Lord God can take on illness and suffering out of love on behalf of another: "Bruno Gröning - Revolution in Medicine - The Rehabilitation of a Man Who Was Misunderstood" in chapter 7 "A Bitter Mission" on page 373.

"The divine law only demands the equalisation of the negativity created by the human spirit. This can also be taken on by another."

That's why I realised back then: I am on the right path, the path of Christ. Bruno Gröning took on a hard, difficult life in order to make the path of redemption possible again. Statements such as: *"I don't suffer for myself, I didn't need to"* or *"There are so many people and it's worth suffering for their sake"* characterised his special way of life. I was able to understand this very well when I saw the film "The Bruno Gröning Phenomenon". In the three-part documentary film, his life and suffering are portrayed very authentically. He said that his mission was for everyone with the following words: *"I have come for all people, regardless of religion, nation or skin colour, everyone is worthy of being helped."* His lectures contain important aspects for the realisation of Christ's teachings and an existentially valuable interdenominational part. His knowledge can also be described as a teaching on the forces and laws of nature. Mr Gröning shows what an important role man as the crown of creation plays here on this earth, which most people today no longer know. He explains how people can access new life energies, how they can become healthy and stay healthy. He teaches how everyone should pass on these powers for the benefit of all life. His teachings serve world peace and international understanding. So in today's challenging times, anyone who wants to has this valuable divine helper at their fingertips. Many people from all nations and religions are already utilising his help.

Then I just asked myself: Who do I ask for help and healing now? The Lord God, Jesus, Bruno Gröning? You can certainly ask servants and instruments of God for help. Bruno Gröning explained this with his statement: *"Trust and believe, it helps, the divine power heals"*. He said that you can trust him as God's helper, but you have to believe in the Lord God. When healing had taken place, he admonished people not to thank him, but to thank the Lord God, because he had done it and he himself was only his instrument and servant. This is a very important criterion for a serious divine helper, that he honours God and gives him thanks.

In the beginning, I asked the Lord God to help me through Jesus Christ and his servant Bruno Gröning. I still do this today. Sometimes I also turn directly to the divine helper Gröning. I don't believe

that Jesus Christ is offended when I or someone else asks Mr Gröning for help, because he works on behalf of God. People seeking
help also turned to Padre Pio as an intercessor for divine help and
thanked him and the Lord God for the help they received. In addition to Jesus and Mother Mary, the Catholic Church has many saints
who can be invoked as helpers in certain matters. According to their
understanding, saints are people who led an exemplary Christian lifestyle during their lifetime and were considered to be particularly
strong in their faith. There are different types of saints, such as
emergency helpers, patron saints, patrons and religious saints. However, there are also blessed saints outside the church who are able to
help people during their lifetime and beyond when they are invoked.

There are many people on earth who ask God, a higher authority,
for help or healing. However, not every religion has a saviour. There
are also people who perhaps do not believe in God at all or do not
belong to any denomination. I assume that every healing given by
God always goes through a mediator or transformer, even if the healed person is not aware of it. The divine pure energy is far too strong
for a human being to be able to bear it alone.
Everyone can choose their own personal spiritual path, because
there are plenty of them. If a person asks for help in their heart and
wants what is good, they will be guided. Everyone is picked up where
they are spiritually in order to be able to develop further. Everyone
must convince themselves of the truth. If a friend has chosen a path
that we do not understand or accept, it may still be exactly the right
one for them. No path is too small for the Lord God if he can only
draw one soul to himself through it. That is why we should have
enough tolerance to allow each seeker to have their own experience.
We can only recognise whether it is a good, divine path once we
have tested it ourselves.

"Find the courage to convince yourself of everything,
feel how your self-confidence grows."

Chapter 4
So close to heaven

After the information lecture, I had a completely different feeling in my body. Completely new sensations of lightness, joy and happiness carried me through the next few weeks. The great lack of energy that I had suffered from for 4 years gave way to a feeling of strength and drive. I also regained a healthy appetite. I could eat with pleasure, which made my life much nicer and gave me a better quality of life. I realised more and more that my body was showing me what it needed in terms of food. Whereas I had previously put together my menu with my head, I was increasingly guided by my "appetite for something".

After my first experiences, I often read the books and writings of Grete Häusler-Verlag and other publishers. It made me feel very good.

Now, of course, I wanted to check whether I could also receive the good divine healing power on my own. Bruno Gröning calls this "Einstellen" / "Tuning in to divine reception." To do this, it is necessary to empty yourself inwardly. This means mentally throwing out all worries and thoughts of illness, everything that would burden and occupy you. Just as we empty our rubbish bin in the kitchen every day, we should also mentally empty our souls of unpleasant thoughts on a regular basis to make room in our hearts for the good. This is because we absorb power with our heart via our feelings and emotions. We open our heart and hands, so to speak. The physical posture should be open, i.e. put your legs side by side and place your hands on your thighs to ask God for healing power. I did this and I felt that pleasant, subtle flow and tingling in my feet again, which I also experienced during the info talk. I therefore took a closer look at my feet and noticed that the two warts I had on the sole of my left foot had become much smaller. Two weeks later they had disappeared completely. This was very impressive for me because I had had the warts for several years and they could not be removed with medical measures. "Wow", I was thrilled.

I also really enjoyed going to the regular meetings. I always absorbed a lot of good energy with wonderful music and explanations from Bruno Gröning's lectures with the aim of staying on the good path. The leader, who came from the Sauerland region, often introduced us to healed people who told us very convincingly about their help and healings. This resulted in some valuable friendships. Walking the spiritual divine path with like-minded people strengthens us and does us good.

I was also drawn to conferences in Germany, Austria and Switzerland, which were organised by Grete Häusler. I remember a conference in Switzerland where so much love was poured out that afterwards I had the feeling of being completely free from evil. It was like being in another world where negative vibrations could no longer reach me. If someone had slapped me in the face, I would have just laughed. This state reminded me of the film "The Miracles of Celestine", where the main characters were several times in such a strong energy field that they could not be seen and attacked by the enemies. My elevated state lasted for a week, then suddenly everyday life returned and the spiritual protective wall became thinner. So I realised that I had to absorb a lot of good energy if I wanted to make progress. I did just that and used every opportunity to recharge myself positively.

I will describe a few more impressive healings of myself and my husband to make it clear that thoughts, feelings, beliefs and faith have a great influence on our health, and that this good divine healing power really does exist, which knows no "incurable".

I had been plagued by back pain and spondylolisthesis for 8 years. I wished with all my heart to be cured of it. One day, as I was cheerfully walking from the car park to work, a very painful lightning bolt shot up my thoracic spine to my pelvis. I stopped, broke out in a sweat, but immediately "switched" internally to regulation and healing. I took a deep breath. The pain and profuse sweating subsided. I still felt a slight pulling pain in my right hip and groin area throughout the day, but I was sure that something unpleasant had been released from my back, which was then confirmed.

I intuitively put this down to the fact that I was simply looking to the future with positive expectations again, which was not the case before the lecture. I just knew inside that everything would be fine now and I was already visualising the future with my wishes: "I'll be completely healthy, I'll meet a partner here with whom I can share these experiences, now I can become a helper"... and I was sure that this would happen. I was really totally positive. Before I had these beautiful experiences, I felt anxious and blocked. Mental and spiritual blockages, fears and a life that is perceived as very difficult can also cause blockages, pain and disorders in the spine. At least that's how it was for me. Thanks to my faithful, positive attitude, I was also able to resolve this physically. Weeks later, I experienced severe pain in my entire back for another three days. It felt like lumbago, I could hardly hold myself up straight. I hadn't expected this, but the circle leader cheered me up: "Something else is being cleansed in your body, hold on in faith, you're adjusting to the healing power, it'll be fine." It was really hard for me to believe that these were supposed to be cleansing processes, as everything felt even worse than before. But then I put my faith in it and as quickly as the pain had come, it went away again. I had a liberated feeling in my entire back area, which remained and I was overjoyed to have come a little closer to the health I had been striving for.

To explain this to you: Mr Gröning calls the different sensations after the absorption of energy until healing "Regelung" / "regulation". The body cleanses and regulates itself, and pain, sweating, skin rashes and diarrhoea can also occur until healing has taken place. This phase must be endured with faith. Then the good is stronger, the burden must give way and the person becomes healthy.

I also developed a herpes on my lower lip, which had appeared a few times a year since puberty. Three months after the information lecture, the herpes flared up again very violently; the affected area extended to the centre of my chin. My work colleagues seriously advised me to go to the doctor. But I wasn't afraid at all, for me these were cleansing processes. I could firmly believe and trust that the herpes no longer belonged to me. After all, I had inwardly separated myself from it. And that's how it was. Everything we believe in happens. Bruno Gröning said: *"He who can hold on to true, divine faith, wins."* My mental state also stabilised more and more.

During the powerful and fulfilling sessions, I often had to cry a lot, I had real crying fits. Everything negative that had built up in my soul over the years was now cleansed. I felt nothing but happiness.

One day, while I was at work, I developed severe menstrual cramps. It was almost unbearable. I was only able to tune in / "Einstellen" briefly and ask for help. But it didn't get any better. Then I drank a hot tea and took a Dysmenalgit tablet, which usually helped. But this didn't have any soothing effect either - strange. By now, two hours had passed. I called a friend and asked her to "Einstellen" / tune in to the divine reception. Her husband and she immediately tuned in to me for about five minutes, meaning that they both absorbed healing energy with me. After this short period of time, the pain was as if cut off, spontaneously gone. That was a really great experience for me.

After a year of belonging to the circle of friends, my hormone balance was also in order, which had been completely out of balance for a long time and could not be regulated with tablets.

For many years I had pain in my left knee, which occurred when I had to climb stairs or when walking steadily downhill. For example, when hiking. The orthopaedist diagnosed that the kneecap was sitting too high and prescribed me a knee support, which gave me more support in the knee joint and alleviated the pain. However, the symptoms did not change. In 1990, I took part in a hiking week in Filzmoos in the summer. One day we hiked up the south face of the Dachstein and took a break. On the descent I got the usual knee pain again. But I felt very strong, stamped my foot and said to myself: "I can walk". The pain was instantly gone and I was able to make the steep descent without any problems. The pain has never returned in all 34 years. That sounds incredible, but it's the truth.

After moving from Herford to Bavaria in 1999, where I had lost a lot of strength, I developed thick finger joints. It really wasn't nice. In the morning I felt extreme stiffness in my finger joints and some of them were visibly thicker. Lack of strength is a good breeding ground for illness. And thoughts such as worry, fear, pity, sadness, anger, rage and stress are negative energies with negative information. If we have absorbed them, these negative forces can cause disorders, as was the case with me. The doctor diagnosed a slightly elevated gout level. I don't even remember if he prescribed anything for it.

I realised what I had to do now: "Don't accept the diagnosis and hand it over to Jesus, to the servant Bruno Gröning and take a lot of strength". That's what I did and believed; I wanted to get rid of the illness at all costs. When I woke up in the morning and could hardly bend my fingers again, I found it hard to believe that it would be okay. I kept telling myself in my mind: "I can bend my fingers" and emotionally went into the feeling of being able to move them completely freely. Or I kept thinking that everything was redeemed by Jesus, everything had already been taken care of, he forgives me, I believe. After three months the haunting was over, my ten fingers have been fully mobile again ever since. That was 25 years ago now.

Another example: About 15 years ago, I noticed a light brown spot on my left temple between my eye and my hairline. It developed into a light-coloured birthmark about 1 mm high and 8 mm in diameter. It looked so perfectly constructed that it would probably remain there for the rest of my life. My GP diagnosed a keratoma. He said it wasn't malignant, but advised me to have it removed by a surgeon. I asked meekly if it wasn't possible for it to go away on its own. He firmly denied this, adding that it could become even bigger.

Now I was sitting at home with the addresses of two surgeons and wondering what to do. I definitely didn't want to keep it on my face because it was clearly visible. Because it wasn't malignant, I decided to wait six months before having an operation. I thought back to what the doctor had said: "No, there's no way the keratoma will go away on its own. "I felt anger or resistance welling up inside me, because Bruno Gröning's motto is: *"There is no such thing as incurable, God is the greatest doctor."* I felt much better, I said to myself, so I'd better believe it. No sooner said than done - at that moment I was able to completely detach myself from it internally, to erase it from my heart and my consciousness. Emotionally, it was as if I no longer had it, even though it was still visibly enthroned on my face. At the same moment I gave it up, the spot started to itch. I knew: "Aha, something is already happening." I stuck a small picture of Bruno on the spot so that I wouldn't keep looking at it. Over the next few days, the spot itched from time to time. I was sure that it would disappear. After a week, the centre area of the keratoma became hard and fell out in pieces as something stony when I touched it. I was thrilled and so was my husband, who is a physicist and was able to observe the effect of the mind on matter at first hand, so to speak. After two weeks, the keratoma was completely gone, including the brown spot that had been there for months.

This was another confirmation for me that if we no longer believe in the illness, if we separate ourselves from it, then it will die or wither away sooner or later. It's like a plant that we deprive of its breeding ground. The illness comes to life if we pay a lot of attention to it and believe in it. Often other complaints are then added. The belief and the thought: "I have a keratoma", mentally cements the condition of the disease. Thoughts are mental forces that can hold or release something like hands. If we believe in the disease, we hold on to it figuratively with these subtle hands. After all, illness is ultimately a mental state that affects the body via the soul. Giving up, letting go, focussing on the good, absorbing strength, faith and trust - this is what brings success.

However, I would also like to mention that I was not always able to release all stresses and problems as quickly as in the examples mentioned. Sometimes it took a long time, even a very long time, for the desired success to materialise. Just stay on the ball and be patient, because we are supposed to learn something in the process. This is the only way to get closer and closer to heaven.

So close to heaven

Chapter 5
A life partner, as if made to order

After my first wish to get well had almost been fulfilled, my life partner came into my life as if on order. Before that, I often thought: "How will I recognise him, is he already in my circle of acquaintances?" Because I definitely wanted a man who had had the same wonderful experiences as me or was willing to have them. I had decided for myself that I wanted the partner by my side that God had destined for me. When I went to conferences, I looked at the men on offer. But somehow I had the feeling that the right one wasn't there yet. I approached Grete Häusler about this matter. She confirmed my feeling and advised me to take in a lot of good energy and trust. That's what I did and I didn't find it difficult at all in this matter. I had positive thoughts and feelings in my heart like: "Let's see how this will work out, I'm looking forward to it." I was so happy that I could trust.

After a year, I began to doubt whether I didn't have to actively do something to meet my soul mate. These thoughts were fuelled when my sister's godmother came to visit my parents. I was in the hallway and heard her say to my mum in the dining room: "Lisa, make sure you don't keep two old aunts in the house." She was referring to my twin sister and me; we were 28 years old and still living in our parents' house at the time. Her words stung my heart. I realised that I was starting to justify myself to myself: "After all, I had to get better first." But I quickly regained my composure, walked over to them confidently and interjected: "My partner will come at the right time, I believe it!" The thought made me feel good. During this time, my sister and I went to a disco again after a long time. In the past, we had done this very often and enjoyed it. I soon realised that I wasn't going to meet my partner here. It was strange, I felt like a stranger in my usual environment. I was standing at the bar, with a good-looking, well-groomed man sitting on a bar stool next to me. He kept looking at me and then suddenly asked if I could take my foot off his shoe. It was probably also a sign that my feet were generally not in the right place. Within the next 6 months, I had regained confidence in my partnership. Sometimes thoughts of doubt still wanted to come, but I thought to myself that these could only be tests and that I wouldn't let them irritate me. After all, I had no choice but to believe and trust.

I had the opportunity to support the then leader of the circle by telling interested people about this healing method. I was given the address of a lady who was suffering from depression and stomach problems. I visited her and told her about the natural healing method. We were alone in the living room, only the cat sitting on the table was still present. During the conversation, a pleasant vibration spread and the lady was very moved, started to cry and visibly felt better after the conversation. I invited her to the next meeting. Over the next few days, she kept telling her son how impressed she was and that she was already feeling much better. However, she had also completely misunderstood some things, for example that sick people were prayed for during meetings and that the dead had already been resurrected. I smiled, because I hadn't told her that. Her son was naturally very sceptical and worried about whether everything was above board here in the circle. So he made an appointment with me to find out more about this dubious group.

I had planned to talk to him for about two hours, but things turned out quite differently. I first told him about this natural spiritual healing method. He asked a lot of questions, which I then answered in such a way that he gained confidence. After two hours, he began to feel visibly at ease with me. The hours passed and we also talked about private matters. For a moment, I thought: "Could this be my future partner?" But I learnt that he was studying physics and was five years younger than me. "No thanks", I thought, that can't be him, he's out of the question. Because in my mind I had been thinking of a slightly older, more mature gentleman. And a student, no way. We had students in our family who gave the impression that they only wanted to study their whole lives and not work. In my mind, I had therefore discarded this consideration. Then my guest told me something about his life, which I found very interesting. And I heard my heart pumping joyfully, maybe it was him after all. It was now 1 a.m. and we said goodbye with the option of meeting up again, which we did. At that time, I found a cosy flat and my boyfriend helped me furnish it. We got on well and I finally felt free in this relationship, the issue of addiction was over. But it wasn't quite clear yet whether he would also follow my spiritual path. I asked the Lord God, if he had chosen this man for me, to guide everything for the best. So I was able to let go of this issue completely and trust. Over time, it became increasingly clear that he was the right partner for my life.

After a year, we got engaged. When I was at a training week of the circle afterwards, I was approached quite openly by an acquaintance: "Petra, that's great that you've found your soul mate." At that moment, I got a lot of healing current in my feet, so that I was bouncing back and forth on the floor. That was really noticeably impressive for me, I felt it was an approval from the divine side. Six months later, we decided to get married. There was some opposition from my fiancé's family. He was advised to finish his studies first and to reconsider whether he was completely sure of his decision. My fiancé was. Shortly afterwards, he lost his engagement ring while jogging. He only noticed when he had already run a kilometre. There was a thin layer of snow on the tarmac path. So the chances of finding the ring again were not good. My fiancé got the idea to ask God: "If you intended this woman for me, let me find the ring." He found it and we got married in August 1992. We then experienced many wonderful things together and overcame many a challenge on our journey through life. So my second wish came true.

What was very remarkable for us was that after the first joint power intake with my current husband's mother, it became apparent over the next few days that her Persian cat had solid faeces, which had not been the case before. Even as a young animal he suffered from liquid faeces. Since this meeting, at which the cat sat on the table, he has become and remained free of it.

My husband was cured of his allergic asthma 2 years after the first intake, which was medically documented. It was interesting to note that the symptoms changed on the way to healing. While the runny nose and breathlessness occurred several times a year for decades, it was only once after giving up the strain and the daily power intake, but it was very severe. In the second year it was so bad that he went to see a doctor. He did a blood and provocation test, but was astonished to find no allergens or reactions. So my husband knew that these conditions no longer had anything to do with illness, but were in fact reactions to changes in behaviour that would lead to healing. And so it was.

Then, at the age of 33, he experienced the same pain in his left knee that he first had during his time in the army. It was a dull, drilling pain that occurred in a sitting position and was relieved by movement. The orthopaedic surgeon at the time diagnosed incipient wear and tear based on the X-ray and said that he would have major problems with his knee as he got older. He even advised my husband to avoid strenuous activities such as hiking or skiing and to use a walking stick to relieve the strain on his knee, which would certainly be his constant companion from the age of forty. That really wasn't a good prospect. Prescribed measures such as ointments and electrical stimulation brought him relief for a few years, so that it no longer bothered him. The doctor's words came back to my husband's mind when he felt the nagging knee pain. He spontaneously said to himself: "I won't accept this diagnosis, get rid of it!" But the conditions worsened over the next six months, even occurring at night. One evening it was so severe that he had to get up because the pain persisted when lying down despite changing position. Sitting in the chair, my husband looked at the picture of Bruno Gröning and with all determination transferred the burden to him and absorbed the healing current. He felt the power flowing intensely through his body. The pain became even stronger for a short time, but for him this was a sign that the healing power was working. He continued to concentrate on absorbing the power and on his body. After about 20 minutes, the pain slowly subsided. He was then immediately able to go to sleep. Since then, the pain was completely gone and has never recurred in all these years. The doctor's predictions did not materialise. My husband skis and we really enjoy hiking in the mountains. These personal experiences were very impressive for him as a physicist to experience for himself how strongly thoughts affect the body.

There are not only angels in heaven (the spiritual world), but also on earth. Everyone can be a helper, an angel, to others.

Chapter 6
Being a helper to others,
passing on love and healing power from the heart

At the end of the information lecture, I asked Grete Häusler why we should make an effort for other people (giving a burden to the needy, sending a healing current / "Heilstrom", believing). I had the idea that everyone had to come to the realisation themselves. She just looked at me with a smile and said: "It's nice when you can help others." To which I was then unable to reply.

I hadn't been around that long when my mum mentioned that her cousin was dying. I got my mum's picture album and asked her to show me a picture of her cousin. I took it out and prayed intensely in my basement room for this person I didn't know. I asked the Lord God from the bottom of my heart to help her in this situation. I tuned into the healing current / "Heilstrom", first for myself and then I sent her this power and a lot of love and light from my praying heart. I felt the energy flowing very strongly in my body, stronger than if I had only received power for myself. I was very sure that this good sending would be passed on to her. My mum told me that she had died very peacefully with a smile. I was very happy about this and felt motivated to continue praying for others.

A colleague of mine at work had had problems with her left knee for years. She was considered to be out of therapy and was about to have an operation. I asked for the healing current for her and after about two weeks her knee was free of pain. The operation was no longer necessary. My colleague was overjoyed and her doctor was totally amazed that her knee had spontaneously become pain-free.

I had never experienced such miracles before the information lecture, I was really thrilled. I realised that the loving thoughts, words, wishes and healing power I send via the spiritual path actually arrive and work. Bruno Gröning let people know: When our soul vessel is full of this good divine power, it passes on to the next person for whom we pray. He explained that we have the function of a small transmitter. He also frequently admonished people to pay very careful attention to their thoughts. Thoughts are spiritual forces; the good ones have a positive effect, the bad ones a negative one, which I experienced more and more clearly in the following years.

The husband of another colleague suffered from chronic joint inflammation. He repeatedly suffered severe bouts of inflammation, so he was admitted to a specialised clinic in Sendenhorst, where he was treated according to all the rules of the art. But his fate seemed to be sealed. He was already in a wheelchair and the doctors gave him no hope of recovery. My colleague worriedly told me almost every day that her husband would love to get well again. I could no longer remain silent.

I told her about my healings and that there was natural spiritual help available. I gave her an information booklet about Bruno Gröning's spiritual healing method for her husband and encouraged her that everything could be all right again and that under no circumstances should they accept the diagnosis. I felt a real resistance and fighting spirit in me: "I won't accept the diagnosis, I believe and trust in divine help and grace that this man will be completely well again." I asked God, Jesus and the helper Bruno Gröning for help and healing in this matter. Every day I interceded for this man and faithfully sent him healing energy and love from my heart. My colleague's husband read through the information booklet with interest. This strengthened his faith, because he wanted to get well again. After about two weeks he was already feeling better. In any case, there was also positive guidance. A nurse often encouraged him in his faith and talked him into getting out of the wheelchair again. A fellow patient sometimes read him something from the Bible about Christ's salvation. Things improved and he was able to receive complete healing. That was an impressive experience for the three of us. My colleague told me that her husband often read the information booklet after his recovery. The doctors treating him categorised this healing process as very unusual.

Over the years, I have had many more wonderful experiences. I would like to tell you about some of them in a somewhat shorter form. I learnt from my mother that my older sister had been diagnosed with glaucoma. She was given medication for it and nothing more could be done from the medical side. On behalf of my sister, I passed the burden on to Bruno Gröning, believing and trusting that this too would get better. After a few months, the glaucoma was no longer detectable. Her ophthalmologist was very surprised.

My husband's grandmother experienced discomfort after cataract surgery on her left eye. As soon as she opened her left eye, she felt like she had a mosquito in it, which was very uncomfortable. Her doctor was unable to provide any relief for months. After a joint tune in / "Einstellen" with her on the phone, the eye was spontaneously completely symptom-free and has remained so. This was a very impressive experience for our grandma, she phoned her son straight away and told him about it enthusiastically.

In another case, an 80-year-old lady from our district called me. She worriedly told me that she wouldn't be able to come next time because she needed an operation on her right eye. A small lump had formed on her eyelid (I don't remember the diagnosis). I asked her if she had already decided whether an operation was really necessary. She said no. So we opened our hearts and hands together on the phone, received power and asked the divine masters and the heavens whether an operation was necessary. We could both feel a lot of healing current / "Heilstrom" and she felt a strong itching on her right eyelid. We realised immediately that the healing power was already working on the eye and so she continued to observe the matter. Three days later she called me excitedly to say that she no longer needed an operation. The findings had reduced so much that the doctor advised against an operation. We were both really happy.

I experienced the following case in my massage studio: a customer told me during the preliminary consultation that I should massage his big toes carefully because he had gout in them. After the massage, I asked him if he knew why he had developed the strain. He replied in the negative, whereupon I enquired whether he had been under a lot of stress and anxiety. He answered in the affirmative. I explained to him that negative thoughts such as stress and anxiety can bring unfavourable energy and information into the soul and cause illness. I knew that the client was working on a PC. I wanted so much to explain to him how important it is not to accept the diagnosis.
I made the comparison: if you believe in the disease now, it is as if you start a programme in your body, the programme is called destruction, degradation, gout. I advised him to delete the programme by mentally throwing the diagnosis, the inflammation, out of his mind. I also advised him to relax a lot and to believe well, even if symptoms still occur.

The customer listened with great interest, somehow it seemed to have "clicked" with him, because he didn't want a programme of destruction in his body. I then went to see him in the evening and handed the matter over in faith and trust. When he was lying on the table again a few months later, I remembered our conversation. At the end of the massage, I asked him how his toes were doing. He told me that he no longer had any complaints. I was very surprised and asked again in more detail. He told me: "I took to heart what you advised me to do." That was very impressive for me, because the symptoms were completely gone after the first massage and the subsequent conversation. It's amazing how quickly something can change for the better in the body when a person thinks differently, believes in the good, in health and no longer pays attention to the bad.

Another experience that is very remarkable: according to the doctor, a customer's mother only had a short time to live because she was suffering from cancer and was in the final stages. The customer mentioned that he might have to cancel the next appointment in three weeks as his mother's condition was terminal. On the same day, I prayed from the bottom of my heart for this woman, whom I did not know, sent healing power and believed. Three weeks later, however, the client came for a massage and reported with astonishment that his mother was so well again that she could go to the toilet and eat on her own. He said that she was already giving commands again and looked a little annoyed. I told him about my prayers for his mum and he looked at me with surprise and delight. In any case, this spontaneous improvement was inexplicable to the doctor treating him. My client's mother then lived for another two years in this improved condition.

We couldn't tell my husband's friend, who is a doctor, about this spiritual healing method for over 10 years. But it was clear to me that the time would come at some point. When he was bullied at work a few years later, he developed severe stomach problems that didn't go away with medication for months. When he was with us with his girlfriend, he was in such a bad way that he was ready to join us. I will never forget that day. It was a godsend for all of us, because the symptoms were completely gone after the tune in / "Einstellen".

Another time, he was diagnosed as needing an operation on his anus. But he didn't want an operation, so he took the Bruno Gröning picture, went to the toilet and prayed deeply for the healing power. Here, too, he experienced healing - marvellous!

Last year, my husband and I also experienced something special as a result of our joint pleas and efforts. My mother-in-law was unable to walk for five months that year because the bottoms of both feet were very painful and no medical help was available. After my husband, my sister, my mother-in-law and I had a joint appointment for tune in / "Einstellen" at the same time, the pain was gone two days later. My mother-in-law was overjoyed that she could walk again. This is also important to mention: The more people pray together for a matter at the same time and believingly receive and pass on good power, the stronger the effect. The power is multiplied. If two people pray and send good energies, it corresponds to the power of four transmitters; if four people pray, it is the energy of 16 people; if 100 people consciously believe positively and emotionally for a cause, this results in an energy field of 10,000 transmitters. It is clear that in such a strong positive energy frequency, good things are very likely to happen. In the circle's regular, constructive meetings with around 20 people or at conferences attended by hundreds of people, there is always enough time to pray for other people in health, private or professional need and also for all global concerns. How often have things turned out for the best because people have not believed the negative forecasts, but only the good.

Over the years, I have experienced many times that my prayers and faith have brought help to others. It is wonderful to be able to help people in this simple way. So this wish has also been fulfilled. My heart rejoices inwardly every time these small and large miracles actually happen. But are they really miracles and what actually is a miracle? This topic is examined in detail in the following chapter.

Chapter 7
Healing through the power of faith,
the most natural thing in the world
- Scientific approaches are illuminated -

How did I come to write this chapter? I wasn't interested in science and physics in the past. I got poor grades in physics lessons at school. It all seemed too abstract to me, I couldn't relate to it. I thought to myself: "What do I have to do with atoms, molecules, etc.?" After I had already experienced many healings, in 2012 I saw the lecture by geoscientist Gregg Braden "In harmony with the divine matrix". I was totally fascinated and excited, it was a scientific revelation and explanation for what I was experiencing. Among other things, he explains from a scientific point of view why belief has such a strong effect on our bodies. After all, belief or the ability to believe takes place in our hearts. However, many people cannot open up internally if their mind does not give the ok and their inner feeling says: "I can get involved here."

This chapter is intended to help people, especially those with an intellectual mindset, to cross this threshold. I hope that this chapter will help many people to believe in everything that is good for them. Anyone who feels that this chapter is not so important to them can read only the summary or skip it altogether.

In the previous chapters, I have deliberately told you about many healing scenarios and guided tours from my life. But not to brag about them or to present myself as something special. No, my motivation was to make it clear that in my case it was not just a one-off spontaneous remission, but that the miracle of healing has taken place many times in me and in those for whom I have prayed. Over the years, we have clearly realised how strongly the power of thoughts, feelings and beliefs, the real faith that comes from the heart, affects the body. And how wonderfully strengthening and constructive the divine healing energies unfold in the interplay of body, mind and soul. The inner release of stress was also always an important factor for healing. All the healings that I have described, and all those that happen worldwide through faith, are generally referred to as miracles. They cannot be grasped by the mind, they cannot be explained and even medicine is baffled by them. Does this mean that these things happen outside the laws of nature?

Augustine Aurelius already said in the fourth century:
"Miracles do not happen in contradiction to nature, but only in contradiction to what we know about nature."
Mr Gröning explained his work with the following words:
"My healings are based on a power lying within the divine order of nature and not on a breaking of natural laws. Consequently, they should not be described as miracles even if they cannot or cannot yet be explained according to the current state of science."
Waltraud Puzicha comments:
"Of course there are miracles.
There are just no unnatural miracles."

I find these statements very important and central, as they present healing in a spiritual way as something natural that happens within the divine order and the laws of nature. All the healings that occur worldwide in this spiritual way cannot be explained medically in many cases. How is it possible, for example, that asthma, neurodermatitis or osteoporosis could be healed by absorbing the healing current and believing thoughts? The body is material - matter, the healing current / "Heilstrom" and the thoughts are spiritual - invisible. Is there an effect of the spirit on visible matter, on one's own body or on the environment? My husband, who is a physicist, and I looked into this question a little more closely, because the German people are very cerebral and believe in science. If the cures are confirmed by doctors here, that is valuable, but in many cases it means that there is no medical explanation: It can't be explained medically. Anything that cannot be explained always has a touch of the mystical and uncanny about it. Does the healing current / "Heilstrom" really exist? Can positive thoughts and energies have such a strong effect on the body that healing occurs? Does faith really move mountains? We know from psychosomatics that negative and depressive thoughts can trigger vegetative disorders and sleep disturbances, for example. In psycho-neuroimmunology, studies have shown that positive thoughts strengthen the immune system and health, while negative thoughts have a weakening effect. However, recovery from incurable diseases is ruled out.

Among other things, my husband and I were also able to experience healings that occurred immediately, spontaneously or a short time after the heartfelt, faithful giving and receiving of strength. Of course, my husband was particularly enthusiastic about this. We were very interested to find out whether there were any scientific approaches that could confirm the above statements. My husband researched the latest scientific publications and Gregg Braden's lecture was also an important guide. During their lifetime, many saints and healers were and are very interested in having medicine and science look into their work - how do the healings come about? What did physics say back then and what does it say today? Classical physics, which was in the foreground in the last century, denies this quite emphatically. Healing by spiritual means, the effect of the spirit on matter, is still not considered in physics today (even in the opinion of most scientists today).

However, as early as the last century after the birth of quantum mechanics (QM), the eminent physicist Max Planck assessed:

"There is no matter in itself! All matter is created and exists only through a force... So we must assume a conscious, intelligent spirit behind this force. This spirit is the origin of all matter." This statement is also supported, for example, by the millennia-old traditional Chinese culture that all of creation arose from energy (Qi) and is also maintained. For primitive peoples such as the Hawaiians, Indians and Aborigines, this is also a reality. For most modern scientists in the field of quantum mechanics, the evidence and assumptions that the entire universe is embedded in a huge energy and quantum field are becoming increasingly clear. The fact that the cosmos and everything in it, including us, is made up of these quanta[7] is scientifically recognised. Back in school, I learnt in physics lessons that atoms are the smallest parts. Today, science teaches that every atom is in turn a system of many small subatomic "particles and states" (quanta). Quanta are the smallest portions of matter and energy in the reality that surrounds us. They are tiny packets of energy that appear as waves (energy) or particles (matter) and can transform into one or the other. In the quantum world, there is a constant process of reorganisation and transformation between matter and energy. If we imagine that our entire material body consists of countless tiny portions of matter and energy in which a constant process of reorganisation and transformation takes place, the influence of the spirit on matter becomes more tangible. If we look at the structure of an atom, the material atomic nucleus is tiny compared to the atomic shell (nucleus 1%, shell 99%). The empty space of the atomic shell contains the quanta, which are the carriers of energy. In the P.M. magazine of 03/2010, page 2, it says: *"The supposed vacuum, i.e. the space in each atom between the nucleus and the electron shell, is literally bubbling over with seething activity."*

---

7 Quantum - Our reality is not what it seems:
   https://www.youtube.com/watch?v=2nXAZna30f0

These elementary particles are in constant, rapid motion, they can join together and exchange information. The resulting wave-like energies are still active at absolute zero at minus 273.15 degrees Celsius, where everything else stands still. Some scientists assume that this field is responsible for the stability of all matter. So we are made up of over 99% pure energy. Who would have thought that? When we touch ourselves, the body feels solid and material and yet, from a physical point of view, it is as described above. If we consist almost entirely of energy, the influence of the spirit on "matter" becomes even more probable and obvious. The energy of the mind, thoughts and feelings has an effect on the "energy body", so to speak.

The double-slit experiment[8] from quantum mechanics caused quite a stir at the time because it unexpectedly showed that the intentions, thoughts and precise observation of the experimenter influence the result. To put it somewhat exaggeratedly, the result is more or less what the experimenter was thinking. New variants of the experiment also prove that such quantum phenomena occur even with larger masses. So the mind does have an effect on the smallest portions of matter and energy, which also make up our bodies.

The latest findings from research also suggest that there is no strict separation between the microcosm and macrocosm, which physicists had previously assumed.

In fact, the macrocosm is influenced and shaped by the microcosm[9].

---

8 Double-slit experiment - Dr Quantum explains the double-slit experiment:
  https://www.youtube.com/watch?v=ip8cmyitHss

9 The microcosm is the world of the minutely small, in contrast to the macrocosm, the world of the hugely large. Between the macrocosm and the icrocosm lies the area that can be directly perceived by humans, the mesocosm, i.e. the earth, our environment. As in the small so in the large - EVERYTHING IS ONE:
  https://www.youtube.com/watch?v=b6IVtCLzvR0

This is also evident from the properties of quanta, which I will mention in a moment. It thus becomes obvious that the laws of quantum physics are not limited to the atomic, invisible microcosm. This increases the probability that healing via the spiritual path, i.e. the influence of the spirit on matter, is possible within the framework of the laws of nature. 5-10% of modern scientists are in favour of this assumption. My husband, who spontaneously became free of knee pain, also believes this, although as a physicist he cannot prove or demonstrate this with a formula or time-lapse documentation. We have experienced how strongly and powerfully believing thoughts and convictions affect the whole body (microcosm and macrocosm). For the body is an entire system, a perfect created work from which man can recognise how great and powerful God is.

But even today, 124 years after the birth of quantum mechanics[10] (QM), most physicists ignore the results of the double-slit experiment. They overlook some of the profound consequences of QM for our real world, partly unconsciously, but also out of fear, because they cannot be grasped by the mind. This is because QM is essentially based on intuition, feeling and intuition, as recognised by important scientists such as Richard Feynman, whose intuitive heartfelt attitude and inner vision bring them closer to the wondrous secret of QM. If you visualise the properties of quanta, you can feel the vitality of creation.

A quantum can be a wave (energy) or a particle (matter) - it can transform into one or the other. It can be in several places at the same time, appear out of nowhere and disappear again. It can be connected to another quantum over any distance (entanglement) and travel

---

10 The first phase, known as the old quantum theory, began around 1900 with radically new approaches to explaining physical phenomena that were not understood by 19th century classical mechanics.

into the past or future. Truly wondrous properties. Even as a scientific layman, I immediately realised that there is great potential for creation and transformation here. Science wonders what laws and formulae govern the behaviour of quanta. But they don't get any further along the purely scientific path. Like Mr Feynman, we feel that a deeper "understanding" of QM can only be achieved through intuition - in terms of healing, how our faith can affect the miraculous properties of the quanta in our bodies. Every conceivable possibility exists in the quantum world. This means that every heart's desire can become reality. This is also described by Gregg Braden in his lecture: "In harmony with the divine matrix (spirit of God)." He also says that the quanta also represent possibilities. For example, the possibility vibrates in a quantum: "I will get well - I will not get well." Both are possible. If I firmly believe: "I will get well", the following happens: The believing thoughts and feelings from our heart send out constant waves (vibrations) that act like a programming code on the quantum world in the atoms of our body and can change them in the direction of healing.

Thus, the energy and information in the countless atoms of our body is changed by the firm belief in healing: Healing information begins to take effect, thereby initiating the healing process. Not only do the fields in the atoms of our body react to our feelings, but the great field of the cosmos also helps. It reflects back to us what we believe - healing.

While watching the lecture, I felt a lot of healing current / "Heilstrom" and it was as if I could see a crack into God's workshop. Because I have been able to observe the effect of thoughts and feelings on the body/matter on myself and many others for many years, I intuitively received insights while watching the lecture and recognised spiritual connections that probably remain closed to the mind. A few possibilities of "blueprints" in relation to healing immediately came to my mind. As described above, the quanta can appear in the form of waves (energy) or particles (matter) and transform into one or the other. For example, if a person who is afflicted with bone loss has faith in healing and absorbs a lot of healing energy, the light quanta of this energy can transform into particles and reattach to the bones. Quanta can also appear out of nowhere. If this person is a firm believer, enough new particles will appear and be incorporated into the bones - that sounds quite logical to me. If, on the other hand, a person has been diagnosed with a tumour and firmly believes in healing, the particles of matter from the tumour can turn back into energy waves and leave the body spiritually at its ends (head, hands, feet). We know several people who have been cured of such illnesses.

Or another example: there is this great energy field in the cosmos that connects everything. So it is understandable to me that the energy of prayer, the healing current / "Heilstrom", reaches the person seeking help via this energy field. Quantum physicists also regard the energy field as an explanation for numerous phenomena such as telepathy, premonitions or spiritual healing. In Gregg Braden's lecture, I was repeatedly struck by "aha effects", statements that coincide with those of spiritual teachers and masters, where the scientific confirms the spiritual and vice versa. Because true science and true religion do not contradict each other.

The big question is: "Who are we? Are we powerful creators here in the universe or are we just observers?" My husband and I have already experienced that we are powerful creators, through our requests and believing thoughts that have brought us healing and help. But we have also consciously experienced the degrading and destructive power of negative thoughts on ourselves and our environment. So we must always be careful to steer the quanta in the right direction through good thoughts, following the example of Jesus Christ and other high spiritual teachers who were and are masters in the realm of the quantum world. For the quanta are the stuff of which this world is made. The latest scientific publications confirm to my husband that, from a physical point of view, the healings do not contradict the natural laws of creation. There is enough evidence to prove this. As healed people, we clearly assume that the healings take place within the laws of nature because we have experienced it. This knowledge makes us very happy.

In her book "Intention", London-based science writer Lynne McTaggart also advocates that the mind controls matter. Intention describes the power of our mind to change the world. She has summarised 8 years of research in noetics (mentally perceptible) from all over the world and explains: "The experiments suggest that thoughts can influence physical mass and effect change down to the atomic level. At least 40 research centres have proven that there is a constant exchange of information between living beings and that thoughts can transmit energy. It is reasonable to conclude that there is a decentralised, unified intelligence and that, in principle, each of us has the ability to make contact with it - not just shamans, magicians and spiritual healers." [11]

It's simply brilliant! We live in a world where anything is possible. Anything can happen. In the subtle spiritual world, all the conditions are there for our wishes to become reality through our faith: the right partner, health, a better job, financial help, peace, that our earth can be healed again. So bring the buried wishes back out of your inner self and believe that everything is possible. In hindsight, I recognise the wonderful coincidence that I was made aware of Gregg Braden's

---

11 From the magazine P.M. 03/2010, p. 4, p. 5 Can our thoughts change matter?

lecture "In tune with the divine matrix" by a customer. A short time later, I received the book with the title as a gift from an acquaintance. The lecture was also a trigger for me to write this book and for my husband to research the latest scientific publications in order to create a presentation, see YouTube[12] , so that we could give talks together on the subject of "Spirituality and Science".

I will summarise the most important points of this chapter:

- There is the healing power, the healing current / "Heil-strom" from the cosmos.
- The whole of creation is embedded in a huge energy field, it is the vessel for the whole cosmos, it connects everything with everything and it reflects back to us everything that we send out.
- Mind dominates matter. The entire cosmos and everything in it is made up of tiny particles of energy and matter (quanta) that react to our feelings and beliefs. As they have miraculous properties, they have a great potential for trans-formation and creation. These effects occur not only in the microcosm, which is invisible to us, but also in the macrocosm, which is visible to us, because there is no sepa-ration between them.
- The heart plays a special role in the "act of creation". Our believing feelings are transformed by our heart field into vib-rations that can affect the electromagnetic fields of the atoms of our body and the whole world and change the energy and information in them.
- **Feelings can therefore change our world.**

---

12 Consciousness and quantum physics - Our science proves
   the power of the mind!

Quantum (figurative) e.g. Energy/particle of light, electron, proton

An **atom** consists of **Quanta** (particles)

The **building blocks** of our world - earth, cosmos, etc. - are the **atoms**

Bar **galaxy**

People need science to recognise,
faith to act.

Max Karl Ernst Ludwig Planck

The first drink from the cup of science
makes you atheistic;
but God is waiting at the bottom of the cup.

Werner Heisenberg

Chapter 8
Illness is a lack of energy and
a negative mental state

These days, many people complain of being tired, exhausted and lacking in energy. This is a very big issue in our society, if not the biggest. Statements such as: "It feels like burn-out", "I'm stressed out", "I don't have time" are already part of our everyday lives. Almost everyone succumbs to this spirit of the times of fast-paced life, even children and young people suffer from it. It is difficult to escape this vibe. I also notice it in the customers who come to my studio. Many of them look weak, their eyes have lost their lustre. They tell me about physical and mental complaints or that the whole situation with coronavirus and wars is getting to them: "I can't hear it anymore," some of them complained. One middle-aged customer pulled herself up the banisters to the studio with one hand every time, she was so exhausted and sat down on the massage table with a deep sigh: "Finally just feeling yourself and letting go."

I can empathise with this every time, because it was no different for me in the past. I also suffered from a constant lack of energy. Sometimes I felt like a bucket filled with water that had a hole in it. Just as the water continuously flows out of the leak in the bucket, I felt like I had a hole from which my energy was constantly escaping. But I didn't know why.

Why do we lose so much energy? Thinking costs the body system energy. If you consider that each of us takes in or thinks around 60,000 thoughts every day, this consumes a huge amount of energy. And I believe that Germans are world champions in thinking, deliberating, pondering and weighing things up. Many have forgotten how to live from the heart and to listen to their feelings, their inner voice or to scan their gut when making decisions.

Because the decisions we make based on our intuition come from a deeper knowing within us and are usually the right ones. If we think too much, it leads to inner rigidity. Life loses its vitality and spontaneity, the things that actually make us happy. My everyday life was characterised by this. I often realised that I didn't feel free in my life. Worries and fears circled in my head, I found it difficult to let go and trust.

What kind of thoughts we take in determines whether we gain or lose power, because there are two sources of thought or power. Spiritual masters and teachers know that we live between the good divine and the negative source of power. Thoughts are sent to us from both sides and we can occupy ourselves with one or the other according to our free will. We usually do not realise this in everyday life because we often react according to habit and our inclinations. We can recognise which type of thought is currently affecting us by its quality and how we feel about it.

Good thoughts resonate easily, have an uplifting effect and do us good. Negative thinking takes a lot of energy, especially if it is linked to unpleasant emotions. These thoughts are intrusive and we soon feel unwell and depleted. We can consciously reject the bad thoughts and put a good one against them, but most people don't know and don't do this. Everyone has a constant inner chatter of thoughts inside them. Everyone can learn to ignore and clear away all thoughts that stand in the way of their good goals. Managing the inner dialogue, as the experts say. This requires the necessary willpower, but it is worth putting these power robbers to one side.

When we dwell on negative thoughts, we are cut off from the good divine source of power and lose energy. Unfortunately, this is usually the case in today's restless meritocracy. Lack of energy and nervousness are the first signs that our energy levels have plummeted.

Too much activity on a physical and mental level and too little rest sooner or later lead to a lack of energy and total exhaustion. The vegetative nervous system becomes unbalanced. If this condition persists, it can lead to disorders and illnesses on a physical and mental level. The mental cause of this stress and the connection with incorrect lifestyle habits that have led to the breakdown are often not recognised. Once the body is afflicted with painful and disturbing symptoms that have led to the dead end of an incurable illness, the person wakes up. The illness then serves as a way and an opportunity to scrutinise their previous path in life. The person seeking help would like to know: "Why did I fall ill and how can I get my health back?" This topic is described very well by Thorwald Dethlefsen and Ruediger Dahlke in the book "Krankheit als Weg"[13].

The clairvoyant minister of God Bruno Gröning made near and distant diagnoses without examination. He saw the respective spiritual cause of a burden from a giftedness and inner vision without knowing the person. And he also knew that a sick, depleted body has a severe lack of energy. *"Illness is a lack of energy,"* he explained to those seeking help at the time. In this context, he compared people to a battery. Just as a battery gradually discharges as it is used up, a person constantly releases energy through thinking, speaking and working. The daily restless and constant use of the mind and body creates a great deficit of energy in most people, a veritable energy vacuum, which manifests itself in its initial stages through nervousness and weakness. We are all familiar with the state of powerlessness. And intuitively our feeling says: "I finally need a

---

13 Symptoms of illness always send us valuable messages from our psyche. The psychologist Thorwald Dethlefsen and the physician Ruediger Dahlke help us to understand the meaning of our symptoms and use many examples to il lustrate how illness can be seen as an opportunity to find a new, better way to ourselves.

holiday, I need to recharge my battery", which is what happens during this recovery period. But this is not enough to permanently compensate for the power deficit in everyday life.

It is no different today than it was back then: if we are too busy, feel like we are on a hamster wheel or only function, we lose too much energy and lose touch with ourselves. In any case, it is important to pay more attention to yourself, to take time every day to find mental and physical peace, as inner stillness is the prerequisite for being able to absorb new energy. We all know the wise saying: "There is strength in tranquillity", and so it is.

So we have to move against the current from time to time, against the zeitgeist of restlessness, in order not to be counted among the degraded. We are growing into a time in which people are realising that they are responsible for their own health, that they should ensure that their bodies are always freshly charged so that they remain healthy and fit. At that time, he gave people the knowledge of how they can always draw new energy for their bodies from the great divine source of power throughout their lives.

In today's affluent society, excessive calorie intake, a diet too high in fat and carbohydrates and too little exercise are certainly among the causes of illness. However, in my opinion, lack of energy is still the main cause of illness today, caused by negative thoughts such as stress, worry, anxiety and too much activity at all levels.

However, illness is also a kind of mental state because the energy and information from our thoughts and feelings are transferred to our body or organs. As the saying goes: "Anger causes bile to overflow". These explosive emotional feelings actually cause the bile to overflow. Or the statement: "Something has got to me." Someone has been offended or has become afraid that the kidneys will feel this negative energy and be weakened. Or: "Something has upset my stomach." The negative influences of worries or problems lead to a loss of appetite and stomach problems, the stomach feels as if it is tied up. The heart, in turn, reacts sensitively to stress - the perceived hectic pace is transferred to the organ, it beats too fast and stumbles. Thinking too much often leads to inflammatory processes in the body such as arthritis and arthrosis. If these negative mental states persist for a long time, they can lead to serious illnesses.

The fact that illness is actually a negative spiritual state also becomes clear when you realise that gifted people such as Padre Pio, Sri Yukteswar (Indian guru) or Mr Gröning were able to describe to the person seeking help exactly which tangible disturbances he had where in his body. They felt the symptoms of the other person on their own body by transferring the symptoms of the afflicted person to themselves and recognising the cause of the illness. Mr Gröning was also able to transfer symptoms of illness from one person to another participant with a movement of the hand. Sometimes he would also make a diverting hand movement in front of a sick person, as if he wanted to expel the illness from the body, which always happened - the agonising pain was suddenly no longer there. Gifted people never flaunt such a gift, but use it sensibly, for example to awaken a person's faith.

I once watched an Indian film on television. A medicine man made frightening noises and movements in front of someone who was obviously ill, as if he wanted to drive away the evil spirit of the illness. I believe that this nature-loving Indian was very close to the truth: illness has a spiritual and mental origin and can be positively influenced spiritually.

In his lectures, Mr Gröning emphasised that illness is something bad that comes via the soul and can only be cured via the soul. And what goes through the soul - the thoughts, it's all in the thoughts! If we burden our soul with unpleasant thoughts, it is no longer able to absorb the full extent of divine power. The person becomes weak, drained of energy, the organs begin to wither because the soul has a direct effect on the body. The person becomes ill. Mr Gröning said: "Stop, don't go on like this, don't go any deeper! I call you to a great conversion!" As an instrument of God, he stood before the people and made them the offer to mentally give him everything negative in their minds. He literally said:

"Give me your illnesses, your worries! You can't deal with them alone.
You can't carry them, I'll carry them for you.
But give them to me voluntarily, I won't steal them!"

When I heard these words for the first time, I thought: "Who is he to say such things?" Especially as his words were followed by deeds, many people were delivered from mental and physical suffering. This is so unusual for us earthlings, because we are so conditioned to first provide a desired service before we receive any help or reward. He, on the other hand, offers to hand over all our illnesses and worries to him. What is the motivation behind this? The following example illustrates this:

I once had a colleague at work who was in serious financial difficulties for many years. This matter was very stressful for her. She often came to work with a red head when she had to beg her bank for money again. Then a man came into her life who paid off all her financial debts out of love. A great burden was lifted from her. How great God's love for us must be for someone called to voluntarily take on the "debts" we have incurred in life and pay them for us. We live in a creation that has its own natural laws, in which great forces and energies are at work. All the negativity we have radiated into ourselves and into the cosmos falls back on us. This can accumulate and affect us greatly over the course of our lives, because none of us is perfect. In spirituality, we speak of karma, self-inflicted suffering that people have to bear. Thank God that the Most High has placed his mercy and love above the law of cause and effect. He wants us to be healthy, to be well, to turn to Him in prayer. Use this opportunity in your life and release everything. Separate yourself from all evil, then redemption can come. At this special time, Mr Gröning is a guide back to this path of redemption. If we accept this sacrificial love out of the grace of the Most High, everything can become good again. I was able to experience this myself.

And thank God we have a natural opportunity to recharge ourselves with life energy in awareness. Divine power is there in abundance, if only we allow ourselves the time and peace to absorb it so that health in body, mind and soul can take hold again.

Put yourself to the test if you are powerless, feel tense or don't know what to do in a situation. Take 15-30 minutes to relax, to let go, preferably lying down in a quiet place where you are undisturbed: Empty yourself internally (imagine emptying your soul). Switch to your feelings, feel yourself and be fully present in your body-house. Go into the joy and awareness that you are embedded between the two great sources of power of the earth and the sky.

Feel how Mother Earth lovingly carries you and the power of the heavens surrounds you. You are now aligned to allow yourself to be energised and to enjoy. With your heart open and your hands pointing upwards, ask for the healing power and continue to feel and savour it. Imagine how a bright, healing light flows into you with every breath and how it spreads throughout your body. You can also listen to a CD with the sound of the sea or classical music and absorb the energy of the sound or think of something beautiful. Stretch and stretch at the end. How do you feel now? Certainly much more powerful and relaxed, you may suddenly get new ideas on how to solve something. This is no coincidence, because you are connected to the divine source of power. You are welcome to use meditations from my Qi Gong activity on YouTube[14] .

The following chapter is about the great divine source of energy.

Pleiades (Munich Observatory) Photo: Peter Stättmayer

14 Energy meditations in the light
    YouTube: Lichtkanal Petra Ross

Chapter 9
The vastness of the cosmos, life energy and fountain of youth for us all

Just as the ratio of matter to energy is in the atom, it is also reflected in the macrocosm, the universe. Little matter, lots of empty space filled with energy that is available to us. Science refers to this energy field as the divine matrix, quantum hologram, spirit of nature, zero point field. Bruno Gröning calls it the healing power from the cosmos or the healing current. This is the primordial creative power itself, with which God created everything and wants to preserve, revitalise and flow through it. Everything lives from this power: the plant kingdom, the animal world and also us humans. We absorb this power in our sleep, on holiday, during the day, when we have positive thoughts or are occupied with something good.

For the reasons mentioned in Chapter 8, most people have a lack of energy that can no longer be covered by holidays and sleep alone. That is why we need to replenish ourselves. We can absorb this divine power anytime and anywhere, at any time of the day or night, through our asking heart and open soul vessel. We are recharged and revitalised like a battery. Our soul absorbs the power, passes it on to the blood and the blood channels the energies into every cell of our body.

This opportunity excited me right from the start. I can do something for my health myself! This natural source of energy costs nothing and is guaranteed to have no side effects. Strictly speaking, we humans live between two sources of energy, the heavens and the earth, which were created from the same primordial creative force. The earth provides us with food. We can also sense the energy that rises in the plants and trees.

If we stand with our feet on the earth's energy field and listen to ourselves, with a little sensitivity we can perceive a flowing, streaming or tingling sensation in the soles of our feet. Our feet are on the earth and our head is in the sky. With every breath we take in oxygen and the vital energy of the sky. If you consciously inhale slowly and deeply into your lower abdomen, you may notice an increase in the flow of energy.

This divine power is a true elixir of life. If you imagine that everything was created from this energy, you can imagine how much potential, power, constructive and healing information it contains. It is therefore the best tonic and restorative for body, soul and spirit. With a sufficient supply of energy, the entire human body system gradually regenerates and heals on its own. The healing power is also an internal cleaning and purifying agent, but sometimes also a scrubbing brush, to remove the "dirt", the negative energies of illness via the spiritual level. If our heart and our whole being are filled with divine love and power and we live in the awareness of being a child of God, we have much better protection against invisible attackers such as bacteria, e.g. borrelia, viruses (corona) or environmental toxins.

This natural source of energy is a true fountain of youth. You feel almost rejuvenated when you consciously dwell on good thoughts and enter this positive energy field mentally and emotionally more often. I feel recharged, more relaxed and more beautiful after every tune-in / "Einstellen". My husband also notices this very clearly. Because this natural force is not just an electromagnetic field in physical terms, but a power pack of emotional feeling that wants to create, build and realise itself joyfully and uninhibitedly. When you open yourself emotionally to this uplifting force, feelings of love, joy and confidence flow into your soul, which fulfil you from the core and make you happy.

Divine love and power are the best means of beauty, because they make our soul light and bright inside. We then radiate this through our eyes and our whole being. And other people see and notice this and feel attracted to us. When I go to a celebration or an important conversation, I prepare myself beforehand and realise that the people around me notice my positive charisma. Something then shines out of you that you can't achieve with anything else. I used to apply a cosmetic face mask before a party, which conjured up a freshness in my face, but it didn't achieve this special inner glow effect caused by the vitalising energy. I think and live in the joy of being a child of God. And if you believe and feel that, then it is true. I also observe this rejuvenating and pure radiance in many people in my circle and in those who practise relaxation techniques such as yoga, meditation or Qi Gong. In any case, you age more slowly because the peace and healing power you absorb has a restorative and rejuvenating effect on your body, soul and spirit.

Here is an example: I read an impressive healing report about a woman from Kyrgyzstan who suffered from facial hair on her chin as she got older. She did not want to shave this area as she would have had to do it every day. She did not want to see a doctor about this because she did not expect to get any help. However, she was very embarrassed by the hair in the lower part of her face, so she wore a headscarf that she tied under her chin when she left the house. When she had been in the circle for a year, she felt the urge to help distribute flyers. There was an information lecture coming up for which a lot of flyers had to be distributed. I am now quoting verbatim an original extract from her very valuable healing report:

"I was there for the first time, took about 200 flyers and had an inexplicable joy inside me. The last time I felt like that was as a child, waiting for my mum. I handed out the flyers "from heart to heart".

When I got home, I felt a great sense of satisfaction because I had done something good. Purely by chance, I looked in the mirror. I turned my head to the side and no longer saw the usual glow from the fluff. I touched my chin with my hand - and it was all smooth. At first I couldn't believe in this miracle, but the next day my children confirmed it. I also noticed that the hair on my head had darkened. I was very happy. I thank you from the bottom of my heart that the divine current, the healing divine power, has removed everything superfluous from my face and body."

This healing cannot be explained medically. When you think about how quickly the hair on her chin has disappeared and the hair on her head has become darker again, it is more than impressive. An inexplicable rejuvenation effect in a 68-year-old woman through the boundless joy of a child and the warm, loving distribution of the flyers. This really is a motivation to live more from the heart, in childlike joy, naturalness and love, because then we are automatically connected to the divine power and look much younger than our actual number of years.

Gregg Braden also expresses this in his book "Lost Secrets of Prayer"[15] . If we were always in good thoughts and only stayed mentally and emotionally in this positive energy field, we would be able to grow very old. Even far beyond the usual age, as Gregg Braden estimates at the end of the second part of his lecture: "In harmony with the divine matrix". These are promising prospects that are worth rethinking.

---

15 Gregg Braden: Lost Secrets of Prayer: The Hidden Power of Beauty, Blessing, Wisdom, and Pain, hardcover

Chapter 10
There is no separation between us and everything in the cosmos. Being separate, being alone, is only an illusion, thank God

How can we understand that? The earth is already so big for us and then the whole cosmos. There is so much empty space between us and everything in the world. For most modern researchers, it is becoming increasingly likely that the entire universe is embedded in a huge energy and quantum field. This is therefore the vessel for the whole of creation.

It is known in science that the universe is continuously expanding, getting bigger and bigger. If you could run back the expansion of the cosmos as a film, it would become smaller and smaller to the point where everything was united in a quantum primordial soup in the smallest of spaces. And when the Lord God joyfully spoke: "Let there be", his entire creation plan began to unfold and expand in a huge big bang with an infinite abundance of energy and information. Everything that was united began to separate spatially and take shape according to his plan. Over a long period of time, everything that exists today was formed and developed - including us. Although very far apart spatially, they are still energetically connected to each other via the divine energy field. The fact that this Big Bang actually happened is proven by the background radiation still present in the cosmos today, which was created during the Big Bang.

The huge energy field therefore connects everything with everything else. So there is no real separation between us and all things in the entire cosmos. Energetically speaking, we are all connected to each other. After all, in physical terms, the whole of creation is almost all energy. Just as a cell is a part of our body, we are a part of this gigantic creation. You can also visualise the great divine energy field as an energy network in which we find ourselves or are woven into. By way of comparison, when a spider moves in one place in its web, the whole web starts to vibrate. It is the same with us humans here on earth, in this cosmos. The way we think, speak, feel, our convictions and beliefs not only have an energetic effect on our bodies, but also radiate into our environment, into the cosmos and move the world. These assumptions, which have already become knowledge for my husband and other modern researchers, change everything. It is very significant and almost revolutionary.

Bruno Gröning said at the time that when a person is healed here on earth, it goes out into the cosmos. He was probably referring to the liberating feeling of redemption. Everything we send out into the cosmos is returned to us according to the law of cause and effect - of sowing and reaping. This is also confirmed today by the latest science, as the great divine energy field acts like a mirror surface. It reflects back to us everything we have sent out or done in our thoughts, words and feelings.

We can assume that we are co-creators and designers in this world, in the place where we are. This gives me a liberating feeling and should also give you the feeling of not being helplessly at the mercy of everything that happens on this earth. No, in the awareness of being a child of God, a co-creator, we can set a lot of good in motion in the private and global sphere, wherever help is needed. Once you have consciously experienced the positive effect of asking and believing, you awaken from your slumber and realise that you are a living, pulsating part of the whole of creation.

I would like to cite a few more examples from myself and other personalities that demonstrate the interconnectedness of all things in the cosmos.

A personal experience in spring 2021, which also fits in with this theme of connectedness, really amazed my husband and me. We were sitting in our kitchen having breakfast. At 9.00 a.m. I switched on the radio, a Catholic service was being held. I listened devoutly to the priest's words. During the service, he began to bless with the lit incense burner. You could tell by the sound that he was waving this vessel back and forth. Suddenly our kitchen was filled with delicately scented incense, as if we were at the church mass. I asked my husband in amazement whether he could smell this fragrance too. He confirmed this and was just as amazed as I was. I love the smell of incense, so I felt this experience was a godsend. When you realise that we were in our house at the time and that the mass took place many kilometres away from us, it's proof that there was no longer any physical separation between us or that it had been overcome.

A friend who had read Baird Spalding's book "The Lives and Teachings of the Masters in the Far East" had a similar experience. She asked the masters: "If you really exist, why don't you show yourselves?" Soon afterwards, she smelled an unearthly, wonderful fragrance on and around her. She looked in all directions, but there was no one around her and no perfumery that could have explained this odour. Inwardly excited, she realised that this was a fragrance greeting from the masters. When she met one of her flatmates at the nurses' home shortly afterwards, she spontaneously said: "For God's sake, what perfume have you got there, where did you get a splash of that heavenly scent?" This statement confirmed her suspicions, but she didn't tell her friend.

In chapter 14 of his autobiography, "The Experience of Cosmic Consciousness", the yogi Paramahansa Yogananda describes a special experience that his master Sri Yukteswar gave him in response to his inner longing. In this ecstasy, he experienced the world from an immeasurably wide spherical view and how his overwhelming joy, his inner bliss, began to lovingly embrace everything in the universe. Here are some excerpts of his descriptions: ... Then he (Sri Yukteswar) struck me gently on the chest above the heart. Immediately I stood there as if rooted to the spot. My breath was sucked out of my lungs as if by a powerful magnet. Spirit and soul instantly burst their earthly shackles and streamed out of every pore of my body like a dazzling flood of light. The flesh felt as if it had died, and yet I was in possession of intense powers of perception and knew that I had never been so alive.

My self-consciousness was no longer limited to my body, but encompassed all the atoms surrounding me. ... The entire immediate surroundings lay unveiled before me. ... All the objects within my panoramic field of vision trembled and vibrated like film images. My body, the master's body, the courtyard surrounded by pillars, the furniture and the floor, the trees and the sunshine began to move violently at times until they all dissolved into a luminous sea - like sugar crystals melting in a glass of water when it is shaken. The merging light and the rematerializing forms constantly alternated with each other, a metamorphosis that made me aware of the law of cause and effect that prevails in the universe. ... The bliss spreading inside me began to encompass cities, continents, the earth, solar and stellar systems, ethereal primordial nebulae and floating universes. The whole cosmos flickered like a distant nocturnal city in the infinity of my own self.

Another example: On 7 February 1971, Edgar Mitchell and his astronaut colleagues were on their return flight from their moon expedition to Earth. They still had 400,000 kilometres to go. As they slowly turned round in their capsule, they saw the Earth, the moon, the sun and the countless stars in the cabin window. Meanwhile, Edgar Mitchell had an apparition that changed his life. He describes the following in the March 2010 P.M. on page 40: "I felt that the molecules of my body were connected to those outside, a connectedness with the universe like an invisible web linking everything together." It goes on to say that some call this a vision, a delusion, the slip of an overworked brain. Mitchell smiles and says: "This knowledge came to me directly, not through my head: I felt it physically." He went on to found the Institute of Noetic Science (IONS), a research centre specialising in thought transference, telepathy, psychokinesis and meditation.

The following experiment shows that there is a global or collective field of consciousness that we can influence with our thoughts. The psychologists Dean Radin and Roger Nelson from America wanted to find out through their Global Consciousness Project at Princeton University whether random generators can be influenced by human will. In 1997, they installed their devices at 37 locations around the globe. On 11 September, the day of the attacks on the Twin Towers in New York, the generators deviated from the random principle in an extraordinary way. The astonished researchers came to the conclusion that the observation and concentration of the world on this event was so strong that even the random generators correlated and showed the same results - the collective consciousness had very probably synchronised them. Gregg Braden also discusses this experiment in his lecture "In tune with the divine matrix". He describes how the collective consciousness field had already changed hours before the attack; the terrorists' murderous intentions were already perceptible and measurable via this field. Scientists also assume that knowledge about a collective field of consciousness (morphic field) is available globally. For example, numerous important scientific discoveries were made almost simultaneously by different scientists in different places. It is impressive how much each and every one of us is connected to the whole of creation.

The Milky Way, Arches National

View of the Milky Way

Chapter 11
Your feeling is the language that the cosmos and everything in it understands

Our heart not only has the task of beating around 100,000 times a day and supplying the body with blood and nutrients via the circulatory system. The heart is also known to be the place where love lives. We also express this by carrying our loved ones in our hearts. Not physically, but spiritually, we give them this place in our hearts. When we think of them, it becomes light and warm in our hearts; we feel connected to these people.

But what most people don't realise: Scientists at the HeartMath Institute California have discovered that our heart is surrounded by a large electromagnetic field that has a diameter of around 2.5 metres. Gregg Braden writes about this in his report: "The heart has its own brain and consciousness."[16] Our heart serves as a mediator that converts all our emotions and beliefs into electrical and magnetic waves and transmits them beyond our body to our environment. These vibrations from the electromagnetic field of our heart act like a programming code on the material physical world and can change the energy and information in the atoms. The cosmos and everything in it are also permeated by electromagnetic fields. Everything in the universe communicates with each other through vibrations. The fact that our feelings are the language that the cosmos and everything in it "understand" is of the utmost importance to us all. Our heart therefore sends out information and creation signals.

---

16 Quote: Compared to the electromagnetic field generated by the brain, the electrical component of the heart field is approximately 60 times greater in amplitude and penetrates every cell in the body. The magnetic component is about 5,000 times stronger than the magnetic field of the brain and can be detected several metres away from the body using sensitive magnetometers.

Everything in the world is touched and reacts to the feelings from our heart. Everything, really everything: people, the animal world, the plant kingdom, the earth, the moon, the sun, the air, the water, the clouds, the fire - ultimately the whole cosmos. Because the spirit of God vibrates in everything, it is energy and life with which we can make contact on an emotional level.

Young children, who still experience our world in its purity and emotionality, or people who are very close to nature, sometimes experience nature in a very special way.

A former work colleague told me about her holiday in Sri Lanka, for example, that her 5-year-old son came to her very enthusiastically. He told her, touched, that he had just been talking to the fish in the water. This was a very real experience for him, as he had said it several times and still knew it as an adult. The mother herself was also very impressed because her son described it in an absolutely credible way.

Another example: My sister-in-law's twins had been to a church on holiday. When they left the church, they both said excitedly: "Mum, Mum, we've just seen God. A man with a white robe and flames on his head walked through the church." They kept talking about it for several days.

In another case, a well-known elderly lady confided the following experience to me years ago: She had taken part in a rose meditation. The idea was to look at the rose continuously, to immerse herself deeply in it, to feel the beauty, the whole essence or being of this plant. She did this and was so moved by it that she cried. It was a very intimate experience. The following night she slept very well and when she woke up in the morning, she saw little creatures (similar to dwarves) rolling and playing on her chest and stomach. She was absolutely amazed and opened and closed her eyes a few times to rule out the possibility that it was a dream or an illusion. After a few seconds, the apparition disappeared again. The lady then interpreted it as such: After she had immersed herself so intensely in nature, in the rose, the nature beings wanted to see what it was like in her world. My friend described it very credibly, she was still moved and touched by it even after many years.

During a week of hiking, the person in charge reported a spiritual experience. As she kept looking at the mountain world, she was suddenly able to converse with the largest mountain, as if in a vision. She went on to describe that in earlier times people were more in touch with nature and saw angels, dwarves and elves. Soon afterwards, people began to produce figurative objects for sale: Dwarves for the garden, angels and elves in all variations for living rooms or churches. In today's materialistic world, these figurines are intended to remind us or give us an idea that there is also a spiritual world. The guide went on to tell us that St Francis of Assisi[17] could even understand the language of birds. Even today there are people like the clairvoyant Astrid Anbu Witschorke[18] , who passes on her telepathic encounters with spiritual nature.

Such experiences happen when we feel and experience the world from our hearts. Then it opens up to us and we open up to it. Like a friendship that we cultivate with other people, an intimate spiritual connection can develop between us and everything in nature, which can be very beneficial for us humans. On the other hand, we are already experiencing that nature sends clear signals when it is being exploited.

---

17 He who spoke with the birds. A story about Francis of Assisi. Stories of heaven and earth - Hardback - 1996 EAN: 9783780623829
18 We ask you people for peace - Paperback - 14. May 2018

"Let your heart be awakened,
speak with your heart, your feelings,
all people understand the language of the heart
, but also the earth and the whole universe,
you are a part of the cosmos,
it also speaks to you, because you are its child,
pay attention to the signs it sends you.
Trust life.
Be an awakened part of the cosmos."

Petra Ross

Let your heart be awakened,
because it moves the world

Chapter 12
Heart Quantum Leap,
Your heart moves the world

I would like to describe here some personal experiences that have shown me that we can communicate with the sun, the wind, the fire, the earth, the water and the clouds through the intimate language of the heart, that they respond to our feelings and requests.

These realisations have developed and grown in me over the years. I have no proof that this is the case. But the connections between the emotional conversations and the experiences that took place were so frequent and immediate that even my husband and others were amazed. Similarly, the animal and plant world responds to positive emotionality when we send these beings powerful and loving thoughts and feelings. The earth and even inanimate matter also seem to be spiritually influenceable. I have supplemented my personal experiences with reports from other personalities.

12.1 Effect on the sun

I run Qi Gong courses as part of my job. The radiant sun in the sky has often appeared when we have done the 18 Qi Gong harmony exercises together. Before the series of exercises, we bow reverently before creation and ask that we can clearly feel the Qi and the power of the elements. One exercise is called: "We help the sun to rise". We lift it up with a raised arm and a bent hand and greet it. Very often it has appeared and greeted us back, even when the forecast for the whole day was cloudy. When I do my meditation in the morning, when it becomes light inside me, so to speak, I have also experienced this phenomenon. For a long time now, I have got into the habit of greeting the sun from my heart when I see it or think of it. I am absolutely certain that it recognises my loving greetings from the heart. Because this is so fulfilling, I naturally also greet the moon, the stars, Mother Earth and much more with gratitude so that no one feels disadvantaged.

12.2 Influence on the element fire

According to traditional Chinese principles, the element of fire is an expression of spirituality and symbolises the spirit. It also stands for emotionally turbulent states and has a destructive effect. The element of fire also seems to react to our thoughts and feelings, which is very impressive.

I had the following experience: On Easter Saturday 2006, my husband and I were invited to an Easter fire at my brother's house. The fire was blazing, crackling and crackling quite well. I watched the fire and became calm inside. I opened my hands and tuned into the healing current / "Heilstrom" without realising it. I thought: "Yesterday was Good Friday, Jesus has already been crucified, tomorrow is Easter Sunday - the resurrection - now I'll quickly throw all the bad thoughts, words and deeds of the last few weeks into the fire in my mind so that they can be burnt and eradicated."

At that moment, the fire shot up and formed itself into a rearing creature with outstretched arms. My husband stood on the other side of the blazing fire and took a few photos while I was pleading with him. It really was a special Easter fire, because later various animal shapes were also formed. Everyone present felt the same way. We sat around the fire together until midnight, enjoying the warmth and the atmosphere.

When we looked at the Easter pictures printed on photographic paper a few days later, we were more than impressed. We immediately saw a wooden cross with a person hanging from it in a photo with a high fire that resembled a blazing creature.

I realised that it represented the crucifixion of Jesus. In the fire, I saw and still see very clearly burning, angry animal figures. It really is a very impressive picture. I had it enlarged and hung it above the fireplace in our living room. Because pictures say more than words, I am publishing it here in my book for your perusal. Back then, Mr Gröning encouraged people to ask the Lord before taking photographs on special occasions so that they would be beautiful pictures that might also contain good spiritual things. I have a picture of Bruno Gröning where he is standing devoutly in front of his lovingly decorated Christmas tree and the healing current / "Heilstrom" can be seen in the form of bright loops of light. Such experiences can happen when you involve the divine spiritual level.

12.3 Effect on the wind

I also became very friendly with the wind and used its services. We often experienced the neighbour's children making unpleasant noises when playing table tennis in front of our garden. It occurred to me to have an emotional conversation with the wind - to thank it, to praise it for how good it felt when it touched my body like caresses. I asked it to come into this street often and be present, because playing is not possible when the wind is strong. When the weather was good, I imagined my body and the street wrapped around me emotionally; I wanted to invite him into our neighbourhood, so to speak.

I can only say that it was the windiest year for a long time. Playing table tennis was significantly restricted as a result. The wind sometimes behaved really strangely: at intervals, sometimes rather calm, then suddenly strong gusts of wind and then hardly any wind at all. As if it wanted to say: "Hello, here I am again." You can't explain that in words. The divine language is a language of the heart; you simply have to experience it for yourself.

12.4 Effect on the element water

The element of water reacts in particular to our thoughts and feelings. Mr Masaru Emoto proves this in his book "The Message of Water". He shows sensational pictures of frozen water crystals. Positively addressed water (loving and blessing thoughts, words and feelings) shows beautiful water crystals when it freezes, while negatively addressed water forms unsightly crystal formations[19] . If you

---

19 The most ordinary substance in the world has extremely unusual properties that could revolutionise our understanding of consciousness. Water has strange pro perties that seem to contradict the scientific view of the world: it can store in formation, react to human emotions and communicate with other substances.

consider that our body consists of approx. 70 % water, it is easy to understand that a joyful and loving mind has a positive effect on the structure, nutrient content and pH value of the blood, while a pessimistic mind (anger, rage, hatred, fear, stress) has a negative effect on the blood count. Body, mind and soul form a unit and the mental and emotional level also affects the body's humours. We need to be aware of this.

The earth is also largely made up of water. The seas, oceans, rivers, lakes and streams are alive and feel whether we value them or treat them wastefully and carelessly. This also applies to water in the form of clouds. Even at absolute zero (at minus 273.15 degrees Celsius), where everything else stands still, the wave-like energies of the active elementary particles can be measured and thus influenced.

Loving and blessing thoughts and words not only have a positive effect on the water we drink, but also on the food we eat. My grandmother, who lived until I was 12 years old, used to say grace very devoutly before every meal for our family of seven: "Come Lord Jesus, be our guest and bless what you have given us." We then said the word "Amen" together. The meal ended with the words: "Give thanks to the Lord, for he is good and his kindness is everlasting, Amen". This is a wonderful ritual that my husband and I are practising again. The prayer makes us realise once again that the potatoes, the vegetables, the salad, everything that grows and thrives for us are God's gifts, which he allows to grow for our enjoyment and preservation. Our appreciative thoughts and loving glances for what is on the plate and the blessing of the food by Jesus purify and increase the energy content of the food. If we then concentrate fully on the food and eat it with pleasure and joy, we have really done something good for our bodies.

12.5 Influence on the clouds, the weather

Can people's thoughts and emotions influence the weather? Commonplace statements such as: "What kind of weather have you ordered?" or "What kind of weather are you bringing with you?" are intended to express that there is a connection. Sayings such as: "The sun laughs or the sky cries" also give the said human emotional traits and characteristics to react to the emanations of our thoughts, speech, feelings and actions.

Are these just empty phrases or is there actually some truth to them? I am convinced that there is an interaction between people and the weather.

How often have I turned to the clouds with emotional pleas? For example, my husband had started to impregnate the patio stones. Suddenly the clouds rolled in, it was already thundering and a few drops were falling from the sky. This was something we couldn't use at all - the waterproofing has to dry first and mustn't get wet. In a flash, I asked the Lord God for help and spoke emotionally to the clouds, asking them to please move somewhere else and rain down there. With my eyes closed, I visualised very intensely that the sky would get brighter, the sun would shine again and the clouds would move on. My husband supported me in this situation and it actually happened as we had asked. That really was a great help in this situation.

How often have I wanted to cycle to a neighbouring town for an appointment and it was forecast to rain that day? In the morning I prayed that I would get there and back dry. I experienced it so blatantly several times. Before I left, it had been showering and raining intermittently. When I set off, it wasn't raining any more, only when I arrived at my destination, e.g. in the waiting room of a doctor's surgery, did it really start to pour from the sky. It was dry again on the way back. However, shortly before I reached my destination, another rain shower announced itself. When we arrived home, it really started again. These phenomena have happened too often for me to speak of coincidence.

Another example: Christian, a good friend, is the leader of the Jazzkids, a lively gang of senior citizens who still bring a lot of joy to people with their music at festivals and events. In the summer of 2016, they were given the opportunity to play at the jazz festival "Jazz in allen Gassen" in the centre of Dachau. I had promised him that we would come too. However, rain showers were forecast for the whole week and also for the weekend. There had already been several showers that day and it was also forecast for the evening. My husband and I took a large umbrella with us as a precaution. When we arrived, it looked like pure rain again. So it occurred to me that we could ask for good weather so that it would be a dry jazz festival and enough guests would come. No sooner said than done! At the place where we were standing, we prayed to God and communicated emotionally with the clouds to clear the sky. I consciously felt the feeling for about two minutes: it was getting brighter and warmer, the sun was shining. I thought to myself: "The party with rain, that's not possible. Christian is such a kind-hearted person, the sun can only shine". And it didn't rain - after 30 minutes the sky cleared and the sun shone just before it set.

We left after a good hour and on a later walk we saw a picturesque rainbow over the old town centre of Dachau on a clear hill. This was featured in a newspaper the following week: "A beautiful big rainbow at the jazz festival over the old town centre of Dachau." We could only smile and thank the heavens. This was one of many experiences in which we were able to establish a clear and immediate connection between the emotional plea and the result that materialised. An outsider could or would probably say that it was just a coincidence. Whether the change in the weather would have happened without our emotional pleas cannot be verified, as there is no "fate television".

I can still remember well that years ago some farmers called the then head of the district. They asked her to organise the right weather for the harvest with "Einstellen". She would sometimes jokingly ask: "What kind of weather do you need?" In any case, the desired weather always materialised so that the harvest could be brought in dry or there was enough rain for the plants to grow. These farmers successfully utilised their faithful prayers and their reliance on divine healing power / "Heilstrom" for themselves, for their animals and for all their professional needs. Below are a few more reports in which rain was prayed with positive results.

I can still remember one case very clearly: Years ago, my mother, who lived in the district of Herford in North Rhine-Westphalia, kept complaining about the drought during our telephone conversations, saying that it hadn't rained for several weeks and that no rain was forecast for the next few days. When this had happened several times, I asked the divine spiritual world very intensively for rain after the phone call. In all facets, I emotionally imagined and felt in the "now" how clouds were brewing there and how it was pouring down heavily from the sky. One day later, my mum was very relieved because it really had been pouring down like buckets. The earth gratefully absorbed the rain.

In the lecture "In harmony with the divine matrix", Gregg Braden also describes a case. His friend, an Indian, had led him to a special place to ask for rain to end the long-lasting drought in the country.

His friend stood wordlessly in this special place with his eyes closed and his palms pressed against each other.

Mr Braden expected shanties, loud invocations or a ritual. But none of that happened. His friend told him what he had done in silence, which would be the most effective prayer to nature: he emotionally imagined and felt himself walking through the rain-soaked fields and the water soaking into his shoes. He perceived the smell of the rain and felt how the pelting drops cooled his skin. He consciously brought about this emotional state and pretended that it had already happened.

That same day, clouds rolled in. It rained so heavily that the ground, hardened by the drought, could not absorb the water so quickly. The Indian also knows that the feeling we feel is the language that the cosmos understands. What we are convinced of, what we think and feel, is reflected back to us by the cosmos. The universal energy field, the divine matrix of the cosmos, is the mirror of our own creations.

Another example: In the book "Dreamcatcher"[20] , the author descri-bes how she spent some time living with the Aboriginal people in Australia in order to gain an understanding of their spiritual life and their total basic trust. In the chapter "Leading the way", she descri-bes a situation in which she is appointed leader of the group after three months in order to find water and food for everyone. She felt totally overwhelmed by this task and was unable to find any water for the first two days. Her mouth was parched, she was completely exhausted and begged the group several times to help her. However, the Aborigines only ever smiled at her trustingly and continued to let her take the lead. After another phase of inner rebellion, she cal-led on God in her greatest need and asked for help. Suddenly she felt very calm and thought: "The friends are very quiet, it's like tele-pathy, they can probably talk to each other in spirit".

---

20 Marlo Morgan, Dreamcatcher: A woman's journey into the world of Aborigines

She then asked her travelling companions in spirit to help her. Shortly afterwards, she remembered that she had been given a stone by the Aborigines, which she was told she could use as a mouth moisturiser. She took the stone out of the little bag she had attached to her bra and put it in her mouth. She soon noticed how saliva formed and her tongue and entire mouth were moistened. The dryness in her mouth was gone. She experienced this as the first great glimmer of hope and felt a little better.

Then she thought: "But how do I find water?" She asked her friends again in her mind: "Help me! Show me the way to find water!" A little later, the thought came to her very intensely: "Be water". At first she couldn't understand it - "be water" - but then she imagined everything connected with water: that she was drinking it, the sea, the snow, a shower, water in all its variations. She was not in her mind, but had intensely absorbed and felt the element of water in her heart. She then found water and was totally overwhelmed by the experience.

The same principle applies here too. Creation wants to take care of us. However, it is important that we use the language that the cosmos understands. If I only think: "I need water" or I ask for it in my mind, then I only confirm that I don't have it, I may even feel sad. I feel the state of "not having" and am very unlikely to get any. There are many people who are disappointed because their requests are not fulfilled. But did they really believe? Were they already so spiritually enveloped in joyful expectation of what they wanted that it could have happened? Probably not. The original Aramaic translation of the Bible says: *"Ask without hidden motive and be surrounded by your answer, be enveloped by your desire..."* Jesus said to the healed man: *"Your faith has helped you"*, i.e. the emotional certainty that it will happen. Bruno Gröning advised those seeking help: *"If you believe that you will experience salvation, then you have already been helped. Just believe!"* In his book "The Power of Awarness", author Neville states: *"You must make your future dream a present fact now by accepting the feeling of your wish fulfilled, starting from the point as if it had already happened."*

In the interesting film "The Secret", this topic is also explained very impressively using illustrative examples. According to the law of attraction, we attract like a magnet everything that we engage with inwardly. This means that everything that enters our lives is attracted to us: the people around us, our workplace, living conditions, health, wealth, friends, social environment and the situations we find ourselves in. Author Bob Doyle says in the film "The Secret": "Most of us attract something without wanting to. We simply think that we have no control over it - our thoughts and feelings work automatically. So everything seems like pure chance." But that's not true. We attract what corresponds to our prevailing thoughts and feelings, whether these are conscious or unconscious.

We should have desires, set goals and believe in them emotionally. Dr Michael Beckwith[21] said in the film "The Secret": "You can immediately start to feel healthy, to feel prosperous. You can feel the love around you, even if it's not there yet. Then the following will happen: The universe will be in tune with your vibrations. The universe will be in tune with your innermost feeling and will reveal itself to you just as you feel."

A Christian or believer in God can then also add the words: "God willing, may it happen." If a wish is not fulfilled over a long period of time despite the best of faith, it may be a matter of fateful waiting or carrying out. But persistent striving for the good will pay off sooner or later in this life or the next.

---

21 Michael Bernard Beckwith, book: Decide in favour of freedom - discover and develop our soul potential

12.6 Impact on the earth and the "inanimate matter"

The earth is revered by Indians and indigenous peoples as Mother Earth. She is our dwelling place, sustains and nourishes us. The earth also has a spiritual, energetic field and senses whether we treat her carelessly or lovingly. People who know this send her loving and grateful thoughts and include her in their prayers. I do the same every day.

In the course of my many years of experience with energetic things, I have gained the impression that even seemingly inanimate matter can react to feelings and thoughts. During a lecture at[22] , Bruno Gröning asked the audience about his statement that God is everywhere: "What do you think the vase feels? Does the vase feel it when you hold it in your hand?"

The listeners replied: "No!". He continued: "No, the vase does not feel it, but God does, because the vase is made from his earth."

I think that's a really powerful statement. That God is in all things, even in the everyday objects that we use and that He perceives our touch. So He also senses whether we treat the objects lovingly or unlovingly. This is really thought-provoking - the divine power is in all atoms.

I have noticed for many years that when I tune in / "Einstellen", calm down and relax, there is a sudden cracking noise, usually several times a day, at the window, in the drywall, at the cooker or the kitchen cupboards. As if something is relaxing here too, discharging. Perhaps my own stresses and strains from everyday life in the house

---

22 Lecture by B. Gröning in Rosenheim on 7 November 1958

have been transferred to the material. My husband has often witnessed this phenomenon in my presence. When my clients relax deeply on the massage table in the massage room and let go, these discharging and cracking noises also occur. Some clients have also noticed this.

Another thing: I have owned several cars in my life. With all cars, I always had the same "complaint" that a brake shoe was blocked and stuck. I always found this strange until I realised that this was possibly a transfer of my own mental and physical state to the brake, as I had a blocked fear of life for many years. A seer/healer also sensed this when she met me in the shopping street in Dachau and spoke to me about it. Such experiences cannot be proven, but I am firmly convinced that there was a connection. Over the years, I have noticed that my energy field has become stronger. Perhaps the intensity and duration of the thoughts that affect matter also play a role. I think that is very likely.

Bruno Gröning sometimes gave people small samples of how he was able to influence seemingly inanimate matter by the power of his will and thoughts. He was able to switch a radio on and off by holding his hand over it. He certainly gave the command purely mentally.

A contemporary witness reported that Mr Gröning lit a wax candle by the power of his spirit and then put it out again. Another incident: a reporter wanted to photograph Bruno Gröning. But she couldn't take a picture, the camera didn't work, no matter how many times she tried. Some time later, Mr Gröning said to the lady: "Now you can take my picture, your camera is working again." And she was indeed able to take a picture straight away.

During his lifetime, Bruno Gröning sometimes placed a "addressed" tinfoil ball in the hands of those seeking help. He formed these balls from tinfoil paper, pressed a cross into them and by holding them in his hand he enriched them with vibrations from the cosmos charged with divine energy. He gave this ball to the sick person in his right hand or had it given to someone else. It served as an antenna for better energy reception, which was clearly noticeable for most people.

In Dr Kurt Trampler's book "The Great Reversal", the author himself describes how Bruno Gröning triggered a healing effect in his right foot. He took the cane from Mr Trampler's hand, stroked it several times with his hand and said to him: "You no longer need a cane as a support, but now it is your medicine. If you are in pain or overtired, take it firmly in your right hand." Dr Trampler did so and was able to convince himself of the recharging and strengthening effect of the cane.

At the time, Bruno Gröning "addressed" a practice chair or armchair to some doctors. Sitting on the chair, the patients felt a shimmering, vibrating sensation throughout their bodies, a flow of energy, which had a demonstrably strengthening and healing effect on the patients. This was also reported by contemporary witness Maria Bauer. Mr Gröning said the following in a lecture during the Traberhof period in September 1949: "The chair I sat on heals! The ground on which I stand heals! The road I drive on will also heal!" Bruno Gröning's Christmas celebrations were often so sacred and filled with strength that the fir branches he took with him have not lost their colour, fragrance or freshness. This still happens today, if the celebrations are free of disturbances and only the divine power has worked.

Bruno Gröning's influence on matter reminds me of the fact-based "Autobiography of a Yogi": Paramahansa Yogananda. In the chapter "The Animated Stone Image", he tells of the great noble master Sri Ramakrishna Paramahansa, who lived in Dakshineswar. He made the temple image of the goddess Kali a special object of his deep worship. At his request, the stone image often took on a living form and spoke to him. This incident is truly extraordinary.

Yogananda had travelled to Dakshineswar with his sister and unbelieving brother-in-law in the great hope of converting him. After hours of praying and pleading, Yogananda experienced the same thing. The stone image of the goddess Kali took on life and nodded to him with a smile and greeting. The fervent request to the Mother of God to organise lunch for all three was also granted. The brother-in-law was deeply moved and found faith. The book "Life and Teachings of the Masters in the Far East" by Baird Spalding is also a very impressive testimony to the effects of the spirit on matter. Amazing effects and experiences, which the author personally witnessed.

As described, we can send our requests to heaven and the forces of nature that want to help us. However, creation also takes an "emotional" interest in the goings-on here on earth and sometimes expresses itself in its own way. Here are a few examples that clearly show the connection:

Right at the beginning of our tenancy, we had a very annoying disagreement with a landlord. When there was a heavy thunderstorm one evening, I jokingly and ironically thought: "It could hit our landlord." No sooner had I said it than it went pitch black in our bedroom. Lightning had struck us and the circuit breaker had blown. I was startled, because at that point I already knew the divine law that everything we send out comes back to us.

The mother of a friend of mine was treated so criminally and ridiculously by her relatives over many years that it hurt my soul. Two days after her funeral, there was a storm with a lot of damage to the house, which had never happened before. We took it as a sign from heaven.

When Jesus Christ breathed his last on the cross, the earth (creation) reacted. In Matthew, chapter 27, verse 51 it says: *"...the earth shook and the rocks were split open and the memorial tombs were opened and many bodies of the saints who had fallen asleep were raised up."* When the minister of God Bruno Gröning died in Paris on 26 January 1959, there was a violent thunderstorm at the hour of his death. It became so dark during the day that a light had to be switched on.

The impressive miracle of the sun in Fatima in 1917 showed the people that the message of the three children (Lucia, Francesco, Jacinta), which they had received from the Mother of God, was true.

12.7 Impact on the plant world

Some people are said to have "green fingers" because their flowers and bushes thrive or bloom very well. But what is behind this green thumb? Is it just coincidence? Is it the fertiliser? Or is there also a human psychological and spiritual influence on the plants? Numerous studies clearly show that plants that have been given a lot of loving attention - in words, feelings, touch, energy - have flowered better or borne more fruit than those that have received less care.

This is shown, for example, by the following experiments, see P.M. Magazine 03/2010, p.4: Bernhard Grad, a biologist at McGill University in Montreal, Canada, placed seeds in several containers of salt water to slow their growth. He first had a spiritual healer place his hands on one of the containers. The seeds in this container grew faster. Clive Backster, a lie detector expert in New York, measured the surface tension of plants. When threatened or injured, it changed in the same way as in humans in a similar situation - even before anything was done to the plants. Biologist Serena Roney-Dougal from Somerset in the UK showed that lettuce seedlings yield around ten per cent more when they are given a boost with the power of thought. It has been proven that there is a constant exchange of information between all living beings and that thoughts transmit energy.

I remember a plant report from a lady from the Meschede district. Although she had watered and fertilised her Usambara violet regularly, the plant was becoming increasingly weak. The flower looked so desolate that she was already thinking of throwing it away. She took the Usambara violet into the kitchen, where she and her husband opened their hands and hearts to the uplifting music of the healing current / "Heilstrom". After they had been sitting like this for a while, she happened to look at the plant and observed how it literally stood up. The stems, leaves and flowers tightened. After 30 minutes, it looked much better. Over the next few weeks, the violet developed so many large flowers that you could barely see the green leaves. The couple were so overwhelmed by the experience that they showed us the flower at the next meeting.

There is a group of experts in the district who specialise in the effect of attunement / "Einstellen" (transmitting divine power) on the plant world. There are many reports in which the healing effect, e.g. in the case of disease and pest infestation, has been confirmed.

12.8 Influence on the animal world

Pets in particular are very attached to humans. They are connected to the habits of their masters or mistresses through their energetic and emotional bond and are therefore also at the mercy of them. As a result, ageing animals usually have the same physical complaints as their owners. I have been able to make these observations several times. The fact that an animal also absorbs the radiations and energies of its environment and that these have an effect, I experienced in the following incident:

When I told my current mother-in-law about the spiritual healing method at the end of 1990 and we absorbed the divine power together in her living room, her Persian cat was sitting on the table. The spoken words, the good music, the divine energies were in the room and the cat was in the radiation field. After this meeting, he was freed from years of diarrhoea. The breeder and the vet said at the time that this condition was probably due to the overbreeding of the animals and that nothing could be done. But the cat was cured after just one day. My mother-in-law was also much better.

Over the years, my husband and I repeatedly prayed for injured or sick animals in our neighbourhood or in the wild. Here the spiritual help was not so clearly demonstrable, but it always did us good not to have to watch helplessly, but to be able to do the right thing in the respective situation.

When my husband and I were still living in Herford, a friend told us about the effect of her prayers for her cousin's pigs that were suffering from erysipelas. She went with her cousin to the barn where the animals had been lying exhausted on the floor for two days and had been unable to eat ever since. Our devout friend prayed three Our Fathers and interceded intensely for the pigs. According to her, she asked Bruno Gröning for his spiritual presence and help in the barn. After just 10 minutes, the animals began to stir and move, slowly got up and were able to eat again in the evening. The farmer's wife was visibly surprised and very pleased, as she was spared the expense of veterinary treatment. Her husband, who came back from his field work, was also very impressed and pleased with the surprisingly quick recovery of the sick pigs.

Mr Gröning himself also had a big heart for animals during his lifetime. It is said that he healed his first "patients" when he was just three and a half years old. Sick cats, dogs and ducks were cured by playing with and stroking them under his hands. There are reports from contemporary witnesses that animals were healed in Mr Gröning's presence and sometimes from a great distance. Today, the district's Medical and Scientific Specialist Group (MWF) has many documented veterinary healings.

I would like to give you another example of the close energetic connection between humans and animals. Alexandra König, a former client of mine, runs the *Sacred Life Horse School*, where she teaches chi horsing to interested horse owners. In her many years of research in the search for peaceful ways of dealing with horses - without coercion or means of suppression - she has discovered the path of energetic, mental communication between humans and animals. The old way of dressage with coercion was a sign of how humans dealt with themselves: conditioned, very cerebral and striving for functionality, which could not make many of us or the animals happy. Sandra König has rediscovered the good, natural form of communication for herself: feeling, sensing (what does my heart say), trust in herself and in life. She also sees an animal as a friend who is given room to develop and feel good. She shows how a horse can be made to follow the owner's instructions in joy and harmony through its conscious, full energetic, mental and physical presence. Mrs König conveys how much our mental and energetic charisma alone, through thoughts, feelings, our posture and movements, which we are sometimes not even aware of, are nevertheless perceived as a message by the horse. She has studied horse language for years and knows how to bring the energy of horse and rider back into harmony in an intuitive, sensitive way through her analyses and instructions.

There is plenty of literature on the fact that you can communicate with an animal's soul and that a loving energetic influence from humans can promote its healing.

For example, the book "Seelenflüstern" by Barbara Fegerl describes her holistic energy work with animals in a very impressive way. The same applies to Penelope Smith's book "Quantum Healing for Pets": How to gently and naturally stimulate your pet's self-healing power.

All creatures on earth feel like us,
all creatures strive for happiness like us.
All creatures on earth love, suffer and die like us,
so they are works equal to us
of the almighty Creator - our brothers.
St Francis of Assisi

Conclusion:

I believe that I was able to give you a vivid impression that thoughts, feelings, beliefs, prayer and the transmission of received divine energies have a great effect on ourselves and on everything in this world. Such experiences go beyond the scope of the incurable and impossible, they make the listener or reader sit up and take notice and realise how connected we are to everything. They widen the scope of their consciousness to realise that such wonderful things could perhaps also happen through their requests. And that is precisely my intention, which is why I have written this book, so that you too can take up your inheritance as a child of God and have such extraordinary experiences. We are all a significant part of this unique creation. Each of us carries a spark of God within us, an original piece of God. We all have divine knowledge and incredible powers deep within us that are just waiting to unfold. This marvellous disposition is buried in many people, they only live in superficial consciousness, are overly intellectual and are trapped in their everyday habits. But this can quickly change with a prayer from the heart and a conscious life with depth.

If you think about it, we should have realised long ago that there must be something very special about being human. The scriptures of the individual religions already state that we are all children of the Most High, something very special, but most of us have not been able to realise this knowledge. Kurt Tepperwein says: "You just have to remember who you really are." His lectures are brilliant and very insightful, but it takes personal experiences of the heart to be able to experience the tangible reconnection to God - experiences that inspire our hearts and allow us to set off for new shores. Then our soul opens up and the radiant spark of God is released and connected to the great divine system.

Perhaps you have already had similar experiences to mine, that you have experienced healing or help, that you have felt guided by God in your life or have been able to recognise your connection with everything in creation. Then you will be able to empathise with many of my descriptions or feel confirmed by them. Perhaps you are someone who has been touched by my descriptions and your heart says: "I would like to experience that too!" But then you immediately start thinking that such experiences are surely only granted to a select few or the negative side makes you believe that you are not worthy enough. But this is not the case, so I would like to encourage you. If you have the desire or longing within you to experience something like this, then the path is already mapped out for you. Whichever spiritual direction you take, just start, go step by step and see what happens. Your heart and your feelings are always your compass as to whether you are still on the right path. In a guided group of like-minded people who already have a lot of experience, the strength is stronger and it is easier to stay on course.

Perhaps there are readers who say: "I can't believe in such events, I think it's impossible - crazy!" There will always be sceptics and critics or people who are not yet ready for this knowledge. But every now and then, in the course of their lives, what they have read will come knocking on their door again and again until they too want to know more.

In any case, it is an exciting path with new and profound experiences that are well worth embarking on. Then you will begin to marvel at what is possible on the spiritual path and who you really are. It is a huge joy to be able to co-create.

Chapter 13
The radiations and effects
of our electromagnetic heart field

As described in Chapter 11, every heart, including yours, has a strong electromagnetic energy field measuring 2-3 metres in diameter. Our thoughts and feelings, which are also a form of energy, vibrate in our aura and also in this field, comparable to a spiritual cloud that surrounds us. If we have good thoughts and feelings, you can see this in our positive aura. We feel good and our heart field is energized. If we have dark and bad thoughts, our eyes do not shine. We appear blocked and these negative frequencies vibrate in our heart field. We cannot see this, but we can feel it.

If you imagine that this heart field energy cloud vibrates a good two metres around every body, it is easy to understand that other people in our immediate vicinity can be influenced by our field, both energetically and emotionally, but we can also be influenced by the energy fields of others. At school, in church, at work, in the car, bus, suburban train, aeroplane, wherever people are together in a confined space, these heart fields touch or overlap. A sensitive person will be able to perceive, not only by the aura of other person, but also by their feeling, which vibration a person carries within them.

There were many times when I sat down somewhere else on the bus or train when I could perceive unpleasant vibes from the people sitting next to me. If I didn't have the opportunity to take another seat, I thought about beautiful things. For example, I imagined a bright spiritual wall that shielded me or sent good thoughts and love to these people. If you have a lot of people and therefore a lot of heart energy fields around you, you should always carry a mental shield with you. Of course, it is best if we are always full of energy. Then the negative energies can no longer influence us.

13.1 Creating feel-good energy fields and feel-good places

The emotional thoughts and feelings from our heart that we create and send also have effects beyond our heart field. I would like to briefly describe some interesting incidents that I have experienced in this regard:

When I opened the front door for a customer, she spontaneously said: "Mrs Ross, how is it that I already feel so comfortable outside your front door, I'm not even in your massage room yet?" I had to laugh. She probably sensed my love and my intention to give her a very relaxing massage. Perhaps also my sense of well-being as a child of God and the good energies in the house that radiate far beyond. People sense when our hearts are open to them and we accept them as they are. I always have my garden door wide open as a symbol of my open heart for people. In this way, we can use our positive charisma to create real feel-good energy fields in which we ourselves enjoy spending time and our fellow human beings flourish.

When I was at the dentist the other day and had to wait a long time, a gentleman sat next to me, busily working on his laptop. He seemed a little tense. I followed my inner intuition and prayed for him unobtrusively (and sent him love and healing power from my heart): "Let's see if he notices anything." After about five minutes, he looked over at me a few times and smiled. I was sure that the loving programme had had a noticeable effect on him. He was then asked into the consulting room. When he stood at the reception desk after the treatment, he was in a really good mood and said that he was already looking forward to his next appointment and looked over at me with a smile. I'm sure he has passed on this good vibe to his family. I have often successfully sent good energies, love and light from my heart to others. This is a wonderful way to help others spiritually, and you can do it too. It is so easy to do good. Allow yourself to receive good energy and love from the highest level and then send it on. With this knowledge we are no longer powerless, we can help. Our good power is needed always and everywhere. The great energy field of the cosmos, which connects us with each other, forwards our good messages. Everything is received, which makes us so happy and fills our hearts.

The spiritual goodness that I incorporate into the massages also has an effect on my work in the massage studio. I often hear from customers: "This really is an oasis of wellbeing, I'm totally relaxed and calm", or: "I feel like I've been reborn, you have magical hands." When massaging, you don't just touch the person physically, but the loving thoughts and positive emotions also have an effect on the treatment. When I am full of energy and feel good, I often have the impression that this well-being and energy is transferred to the client. There are clients who have left my studio feeling healed, simply because I massaged positive feelings into them in good faith.

For example, a woman came to me who had lymph congestion in her left leg after meniscus surgery. The doctor told her that it would take six weeks to get rid of the problem. He advised her to get a prescription for medical lymphatic drainage. The customer already knew me and asked if I could help her and if I offered medical lymphatic drainage. I said no and offered her a foot and leg massage, which also had a decongestive effect and could help her. She gratefully accepted the offer and came to me walking on two crutches. I was full of energy and massaged her with thoughts and feelings of lightness and energy flow. Within three days, the accumulated fluid had completely drained out of a small open area of the scar. The doctor was very surprised and asked several times what she had done. Just a foot and leg massage and such a quick healing process with this medical diagnosis? That was inexplicable to him.

Tinnitus, headaches, nerve pain, foot complaints and back pain have also been relieved or eased in my studio. Before I start the massage, I pray in my heart for a successful outcome. I then realise that I am connected to the cosmos, that I am standing here at the table on its behalf and that all good things are being passed on through me. I also have a picture of Jesus Christ and the servant of God Bruno Gröning in the room, whom I like to ask to be present with their power and love. This noticeably raises the vibration and I then massage more intuitively and lovingly. Everything we ask for and talk about is immediately spiritually and energetically present in the room.

Indigenous peoples such as the Hawaiians also know about these things. They recharge themselves with energy in the great outdoors. With a chanted invocation, the masseur invokes the aloha spirit, the good spirit of Hawaii, as well as the energies of the cosmos and Mother Earth. He invites them to be spiritually present and help during the treatment. After the prayer invocation, the masseur is recharged. He also feels around him how powerful and healing the energies he has summoned are, which he then passes on to the person in need.

During a healing ceremony, he raises a hand to the sky, mentally and emotionally draws strength from the universe and passes it on by laying on hands. He incorporates the elements of nature and the seven basic Hawaiian principles into this touch. The masseur thanks the natural elements and asks them for strength and support. He connects mentally and emotionally with fire, water, earth, wind, stone, plants, animals and people and blesses everything. Blessing is something special because it means forgiving everything, oneself, others and everything in the world. Everything becomes positive and helpful. In this way, goodness returns in the form of light, love and harmony. He passes on these positive vibrations to those in need.

The Hawaiians sense what deficiencies the person in need has on the body, soul and spirit level and place what they need emotionally into the massage. The masseur or kahuna massages the person back to fluidity on all levels by being the living life itself. New energies, joy and a great deal of love are given through him and flow into the person in need. This restores the client to their natural, original state so that they can once again face life openly and joyfully.

Two more examples of how you can create feel-good energy fields: In the last years of my mother's life, I regularly travelled to visit her for a week to support her and relieve the other family members. It was very difficult for me to close my heart every time I saw how she suffered from her mental and physical stress. My dear twin sister and I were able to help her a little with delicious food, encouraging words and massages - so she was distracted. She also realized that our attitude / "Einstellen" was doing her good and that help was coming in. Each time, my week-long stay also included a visit to church, where I prayed fervently for her. At one point afterwards, I had the intense thought of completely detaching myself from her complaints, taking in a lot of strength and only radiating positivity. Because the question arises: Which energy field is stronger? Does my mum manage to drag me down emotionally with her painful vibration or is my positive energy field so strong that it lifts her up and builds her up? No sooner said than done! But that day she wasn't feeling well at all, complaining of feeling unwell and severe back pain. But I managed to completely ignore all her expressed discomfort and sorrowful looks and to radiate feelings of release, lightness and spontaneity and to act out and be it. It took a whole day for her to start smiling and spontaneously and joyfully expressing good thoughts and words. My mum had unconsciously absorbed the good vibes and felt freer and happier. She no longer complained of any physical complaints. When I left a day later, her eyes shone like twinkling stars, she looked so happy. My sister and I rejoiced with her. The other family members also noticed her positive change.

Another time, when I visited my beloved mum a few months before she went home, she was already very exhausted and suffering noticeably. I sat with her on the sofa and held her in my arms. I thought about how I could raise the energy in the room and remembered Maria Bauer, who had witnessed B. Gröning at a Christmas party. When the song "Silent Night, Holy Night" was sung, she suddenly no longer saw Bruno Gröning on the stage, but Jesus Christ in the brightest light. She and other guests were overwhelmed by this experience. I thought to myself, maybe I can bring some of this vibration into our living room. I asked Jesus Christ in my heart to come to me and my mum in this room with his light and power. After a while, I could feel that the room was becoming lighter and a heavenly peace was spreading. This special vibration was visibly good for my dear mum. I hugged her and held her in my arms. My sister Birgit, who was in the kitchen next door ironing, also noticed this special atmosphere. She came into the living room to see what was going on. Birgit knew nothing about my request. I only told her about it afterwards.

Another experience reinforced our realisation that a strong, cheerful and positively charged atmosphere can have an uplifting and healing effect on people. In this context, Bruno Gröning speaks of tearing people out of their illness. Because almost every illness, every complaint is accompanied by more or less strong unpleasant feelings, which then have a negative influence on each other and from which the person can only emerge with difficulty or not at all.

This was the case for the husband of an elderly couple who were making preparations for their golden wedding anniversary. A good friend of ours had been hired to provide the musical accompaniment. A week before the ceremony, we considered cancelling the date because the health of the golden bridegroom had deteriorated considerably. There were already initial signs and thoughts that he might soon go home. In the end, the ceremony went ahead after all, as he still wanted to experience this special occasion, albeit only to a limited extent. And lo and behold, this elderly gentleman visibly blossomed at this wedding celebration. Our friend, a professional musician of a special kind, managed to open everyone's hearts with his humorous musical performances, guided dances and games. The atmosphere in the ballroom was so relaxed and cheerful that all the guests lost their inhibitions and joined in the celebrations. The golden bridegroom got better and better as the party went on and stayed in until the end. The next day, the wedding couple thanked the good-humoured musician very warmly. The wife reported that her husband had recovered during the celebration, that a veritable miracle had happened to him. When our friend told us this story, he himself was amazed and also a little proud.

In this way, each of us has the opportunity to create feel-good energy fields everywhere through light, loving thoughts, words and ideas, which strengthen ourselves and are also perceived by others as tangibly pleasant.

At home, it is of course up to each individual to create their own little feel-good paradise. You should bear in mind that everything radiates an energy that may or may not be good for you. Sometimes fashion trends dictate certain colours, styles and shapes that you adopt, but which have a negative effect on the indoor climate or your own feelings. So you should be careful when making a purchase.

A painting of nature, for example, radiates a completely different energy to modern art. Which picture gives me a warm feeling? There are plenty of homes in which the shelves are crammed with books, some of which contain nothing good. It's certainly worth tidying up.

Colourful flowers, pictures of nature, glowing stones, candles, a babbling fountain and pleasant fragrances enhance the atmosphere and radiate something positive. Angels are also welcome guests in my home. They are made of porcelain, small and delicate, well distributed around the room. I also have a beautiful picture of Jesus Christ, Mother Mary and Mr Gröning in my living room, which radiate peace, love and strength. I feel this very clearly when I look at them and so I am always in good company. Sometimes I myself send a lot of love from my heart into the room I'm in and the energy level immediately lifts noticeably.

There are so many places where we come into contact with people, where we can radiate spiritual goodness into our surroundings. This allows us to spread a pleasant atmosphere of well-being. I have been in modern and luxuriously furnished flats and houses that seemed cool and energetically empty to me. Because what people have inside is reflected on the outside. On the other hand, the most simply furnished hut can trigger a sense of well-being if love lives there.

13.2 Unfavourable energy fields are also created

I would like to describe a few incidents here of how unfavourable thoughts and feelings have exerted noticeable negative influences on people and spaces.

My husband and I had ordered a desk, which was brought by two men from a furniture company and assembled in the basement. As it was raining, I asked the men to take off their shoes when entering the house. They were not happy about this, as they had to go to their van several times and take their shoes off and on again each time. From my point of view, this was justified; I was also afraid that they might scratch the wooden stairs with their thick shoes. It was only later that I realised that they must have been terribly annoyed. After they had hurriedly set up the desk, I noticed some cracks on the top. I was offered a reduction in the price or to bring in a new top. As I couldn't decide so quickly and wanted to call my husband, they were alone in the room for a while and became impatient. They remained friendly, but behind the façade things must have been simmering. When the gentlemen had left, I didn't feel well. They were probably annoyed that, despite the good discount, they didn't get a tip. I would certainly have done that now, you're always smarter afterwards.

The next day, I went to my mum's for a week. My husband came home from a business trip in the evening and looked at the newly installed desk in the basement room. He immediately felt uncomfortable in the study and realised that something was wrong. My partner hadn't taken these perceptions too seriously that evening. But the next day, sitting on his desk chair, he got uneasy shivers in his body. There were often unexpected cracks in the room and he could really feel that something unpleasant was emanating from the corner where the desk was. When my husband switched off the light on his way out and looked at his desk again, it cast shadowy outlines in the dark that looked like a monster. It sent a shiver down his spine. Shocked by this impression, he switched the light back on and was relieved to see a completely normal desk in the corner. But he could still feel that uneasy, tingly feeling.

The next day, he felt these unpleasant emanations from the desk so strongly that he thought about giving it back. It sounds unbelievable, but it actually happened. My husband is a sensible person who doesn't care for crazy things and when he says something like that, it has substance. He instinctively opened the windows and ordered the negative forces and powers to leave the room and the house. He then absorbed a lot of divine power and summoned good energies for the basement room. The next day, the atmosphere was already better, and after cleaning and absorbing power again, the energetic room climate was back in order.

When I came back from my family visit, my husband told me about his experience. I realised that it had to be connected to the two removal men and I was immediately able to give him a possible explanation. We are both very sure that the negative thoughts and feelings of the two men had manifested themselves energetically in the basement room, which had triggered such a strong reaction in my husband.

In another case, a cosmetics saleswoman came to my house. After the demonstration, I told her about divine things, but she didn't want to hear them. She didn't believe in God. The lady had already had experience in spiritualistic sessions and probably wanted to give me an insight into her spiritual world. She looked at me with an ironic and eerie look and probably summoned her spirit world. Suddenly an old telephone from the past rang. She asked me: "Is it ringing, it's not my phone?" I felt strange and was glad when she left the house.

In the time that followed, I often had the feeling that I was not alone, as if a strange spiritual being was standing next to me or I could feel the breeze of someone passing by. I could no longer fall asleep alone at night and always needed some light in my bedroom. This woman had left something very noticeably negative in the house for me. Something from her gaze and words had penetrated me and resonated with me. This gave me the chance to let it clear up inside me. I prayed a lot to God that I would be freed from it. His son Jesus Christ was able to cast out demons and evil spirits, so I relied on his spiritual help in this matter. It was only after a few weeks that

I felt freed from it. I was very happy about this, thank God.

My friend told me about her neighbourhood, where harmony was totally disrupted. Lying, ridiculing, gossiping and gossiping were the order of the day. She and her husband felt very negatively about it, they had a really bad feeling in their stomachs. When her husband came home from work in the evening and drove into the residential street, he could clearly feel the negative vibes. As if there was a dark cloud hanging in and over the street that you had to breathe in. A stationary negative energy field is bound to form if people are constantly thinking and transmitting bad thoughts in one place.

There was a situation in the life of an acquaintance in which a person had poured out so many mean things on her that she was unable to let go, to forgive. In the evening in her bedroom, out of indignation in her mind, she shook the person's shoulders very emotionally and slapped them hard in the face. That's an educational measure, the friend thought, to apologise for it herself. Her husband knew about the tension between them. He asked his wife, somewhat surprised, what she had done to this person, who was sitting on the chair like a collapsed sack of flour. The person herself approached my friend a day later: "Anni, what have you done to me?" She realised that this experience was no coincidence when she repeated it on other occasions - with the same result. She could not have been shown more clearly that she creates energy fields and forces through her thoughts and emotions, which arrive exactly where she sends them and can trigger effects.

The more conscious we become in this respect, the more experience we have in this area, the stronger the effect. And the greater the responsibility not to abuse this conscious power. That's what my friend decided to do.

If there has been an argument in a room, long negative discussions or bad things have happened, it is recommended to cleanse the room energetically. To do this, open the windows and doors and walk around the room clapping your hands. This will startle the negative energies and then order them out. You can also walk through the room with steaming incense, which has a clearing and cleansing effect. I also often call upon Jesus to come in and expel the spiritual evil or place his image or a cross there.

13.3 The free choice of energy fields

We decide in which energy fields we move. Firstly through our own thoughts and feelings, which we are free to choose. We often don't even realise this and yet we do. Mr Gröning explained that we are constantly sent thoughts from both good and negative sources. This also gives us the opportunity to give negative thoughts the boot and focus on the positive. And we also decide which people and therefore energy fields we surround ourselves with, at least in our free time. Not all of us have good thoughts. And yet we feel comfortable around some people and uncomfortable in the presence of others. This is no coincidence. The spiritual world that someone carries within them radiates and either does us good or breaks us down. Our surroundings, our circle of friends and acquaintances have a great influence on us. Johann Wolfgang von Goethe already commented on this topic: "Tell me who you are with, and I will tell you who you are." That's why you should choose your circle of acquaintances and friends carefully, because you unconsciously adopt their habits and characteristics.

The current leader of the circle said at a meeting that he could tell exactly which friend his daughter was with that day without him having seen it. His daughter had unconsciously given off mannerisms and gestures that he could attribute to a particular friend. His suspicions were confirmed in retrospect.

It is wise to share our free time with people who have achieved goals that we ourselves are still striving for. People whose closeness makes us feel good and who make our hearts beat faster. Where we don't feel comfortable, where the chemistry isn't right, we should distance ourselves. We can consciously place ourselves in energy fields that build us up. Older people come alive when babies and small children are around them. Their natural childlike emotionality revitalises and cheers them up. I like being with young people, simply because the power, the drive, the youthful beauty and freshness invigorate me. After all, I want to stay young for a long time. Classical concerts, spiritual and religious circles, dance clubs, everything that makes our hearts soar, lifts our emotions and strengthens our energy field. However, we can also be energised purely through our emotional imagination. For example, we can enter the energy field of a victor, a redeemed person, feel it, be it. We immediately perceive the strengthening effect. If we manage to stay in this energy field despite pain, we can experience great health improvements or even healing. If we cannot create such an energy field ourselves, then we should go to places where others create such a healing atmosphere. I have often experienced this special atmosphere at Circle conferences. The uplifting talks, healing reports and touching pieces of music bring the participants into a receptive attitude - the doors of the heart o-pen. A light-filled energy field builds up in which healing can take place.

Shamans like to assign a suitable power animal to a person who lacks important personality traits. For example, that of a bear or an eagle. I remember one particular report of a shaman who assigned a 9-year-old boy the power animal of the bear. This anxious boy was often teased by his classmates and friends, which caused him great suffering. The shaman advised the child that he could call the bear when he was afraid. The bear would then come to him with its energy and presence and help him. The boy accepted this very well. When the boy was teased again, he called the bear and it visibly appeared to his friends, causing them to run away in fright. Since then, the problem had been solved and some of the bear's strength had been transferred to the child energetically.

Spiritually mature people can connect with an idol or a spiritual master in such an energetic and conscious way that one gets the impression that the master is working through the person, as was seen with the disciples of Jesus, Bruno Gröning or other followers of Christ. The spiritual connection to their master is so strong that healings and extraordinary things can also happen through them.

Man, Universe, Eternity (Source: pixabay)
As we already know, the great energy field of the cosmos connects us with everything, energetically speaking.

Chapter 14
Special types of connection between people
- telepathy -

As we already know, the great energy field of the cosmos connects us with everything, energetically speaking. In physical terms, this is called entanglement. Sometimes particularly intense entanglements also occur between people.

I experience this with my husband and his beloved mum. My husband has had a deep bond with his mum since childhood and has a really good sense of when she's not feeling well. Then he calls her and almost every time his feeling is confirmed. He also has such a close bond with me, even over long distances, that he can clearly sense when something is wrong with me. There also seems to be a telepathic connection between my twin sister and me. Even as children and teenagers, we would sit next to each other and want to say the same thing to the other at the same moment. We had to laugh spontaneously.

A friend who is a mother of two children told me that her older 7-year-old daughter gets restless and anxious when her dad is unwell, even though he works far away from her. The telephone contact brought confirmation. The extent to which some spouses are inwardly connected and intertwined can be seen when a partner dies and the bereaved person has the feeling that they are losing the ground beneath their feet or that a part of themselves has died. It is often the case that the bereaved person is heavily burdened by the grief and the unresolved loss and follows the deceased. I know of private cases where this has happened. Such extreme entanglements also occur between parents and children. I know of a case where the mother was unable to overcome the sudden death of her daughter and died of grief.

There are also entanglements outside the family, for example of people who carry the same positive or negative life programming from childhood. When it comes to positive entanglements and equality and these people meet, it's just heaven. But when it comes to negative programming from childhood and life brings these people together who have the same negative traits, it's an instructive lesson.

Since my childhood, I had the wrong life pattern in me that I believed I was only valuable if I performed. This pattern has kept me in check for several decades of my life. In my childhood, youth and professional life, I perceived like-minded people as annoying competitors who had to be defeated. I didn't like these people and was often annoyed by them. After I had experienced healing, this changed over the years and I felt compassion for these fellow sufferers and recognised myself in the other person. I realised how I had put myself under pressure to live up to the standard of being the best. I increasingly felt love for these people and asked from the bottom of my heart that they too would be saved from this fate.

In another case, we had people around us who were so close to us that, despite being physically separated, they could sense when we were talking or even ranting about them. This meant they couldn't hear us acoustically. They confirmed to us that they could feel something. Their perception was therefore transmitted to them via the spiritual field that connects us all. But they soon perceived things that they misjudged and misinterpreted. This caused a lot of unrest in our environment.

This incident was the most vivid proof for my husband and me that there is interconnectedness between people and between all things in the cosmos.

Chapter 15
Sending emotional peace and love

"You can only have peace if you give it."
Marie von Ebner-Eschenbach

If you want to send real emotional peace and love, you first need both yourself in your heart. Even after my first healing of insomnia and sleep disorders, I was so filled with love, happiness and peace that I felt an inner urge to pass on this emotional experience.

I met my parents with more love and peace. I was able to give my mum a hug when I greeted her, which I couldn't do before or didn't think I could do. My parents noticed the positive change in me. I remember the words of Albert Schweitzer, which I read together with my father in the corridor of our hospital: *"There is much coldness among men because we dare not give ourselves as warmly as we are."* This saying applied well to our family. It was always all about work and sharing feelings was rare. Everyone lacked love and no one could satisfy the other's longing, which often ended in discord and arguments. Thank God I was able to find the source of love and peace. I was richly blessed and, following the wisdom of Albert Schweitzer, was able to behave more and more as I really am.

Because I, and you too, are all children of God and should fly the flag for love, peace and forgiveness. It really is worth fighting for these goals and overcoming your inner bastard from time to time. For example, I asked for help for people in disputes and disharmony at work or in their private lives and sent them emotional love and peace as soon as calm returned. That helped every time, because the good message reached the next person. In the joint meetings and at conferences of the circle, I heard impressive testimonies from participants who had similar experiences.

I remember a report from a Dutchman who, after his healing, felt a deep need to make peace with a person he hated. He literally said: "I couldn't stand that man, I could have drunk his blood." When this man met him after his healing, he could not walk past him. Out of an inner good urge, he approached him and made peace. He also had an inner need to make peace with his sister. The relationship had been broken off for 20 years because of a quarrel. He asked his wife to call his sister to arrange a meeting. The sister agreed and a good new beginning was made. The relationship became more cordial than it had ever been before the argument.

People from former war zones such as Serbia, Kosovo and the Middle East also reported how they found inner peace again through their healing and the love of God that was given to them and were able to forgive their former arch-enemies. Peace is always prayed for in the intercessions: peace in our own hearts, in the family, at work, peace in the neighbourhood, for crisis areas and for world peace. In doing so, we send feelings of harmony and unity throughout the world. If many people come together and absorb the feeling of peace in their hearts and pass it on, this can change the world for the better. When many people pray for the same cause, these broadcasts are multiplied and the effect is amplified.

Gregg Braden describes a sensational project on this topic, the International Peace Project in the Middle East from 1988: Participants were trained to feel as if there was already peace. These trained people were sent to the war zone in question and together they began their actively felt peace work.[23]

The result was quite astonishing, as peace was achieved and the acts

---

23 Orme-Johnson, D. W., Alexander, C. N., Davies, J. L., Chandler, H. M., & Larimore, W. E. (1988) An International Peace Project in the Middle East: The Effects of the Maharishi Technology of the Unified Field

of violence were significantly reduced. When the trainees stopped their peace work, the violence increased again. The initiators of the project wondered in amazement whether the result was perhaps just a coincidence. The experiment was repeated several times and the result was always the same. When the peace activists collectively felt that there was peace, there was more peace; when they stopped, the level of violence increased significantly. These sensational results were published in The Journal of Conflict Resolution, Dec. 1988, 32, no 4. Based on these results, it was even calculated that if approximately 7,740 people felt this emotional peace, it would be enough to have an effect on world peace for 7 billion people.

For Gregg Braden, too, it is already a reality: we can speak with the feeling from our heart to everything, including the world around us, in order to create peace. These realisations, which are almost revelations, give each of us the opportunity to do something for peace in our environment and on earth. When we watch the daily news, we have ample opportunity to have a healing effect on the negative events (wars, violence) with prayers and felt peace, with the love flowing from our hearts. The evidence is there, we just need to put these valuable insights into practice. And we can all do that. All that remains for me to say is: "Let's do it!"

*"It is a mistake if we think
that we only live in a material sense,
only with the spirit and
life on the outer plane.
We live and work all the time
on other levels of consciousness,
meet with others there
and have an effect on them,
and what we do and feel and think there,
the forces we gather,
the results we prepare,
have, without our knowledge
incalculable significance and scope
for our outer life."*

**Sri Aurobindo, In: Satprem
or the Adventure of Consciousness**

Chapter 16
Dreams are not foams

"Sleep is the umbilical cord through which the individual
is connected with the universe."
Friedrich Hebbel

Everyone dreams almost every night, but most people can't remember them in the morning. Many everyday things are processed during the night and are reflected in dreams.

Each of us has probably had nightmares in which inner fears or unpleasant experiences suddenly involve us in a horror film in our dreams. We are glad when we wake up in the morning and realise that - thank God - it was only a dream. There are people who have had such a traumatic experience in their lives that they dream about this terrible experience almost every night and wake up in a cold sweat. A shock experience like this is programmed in and is difficult to treat and heal with psychotherapy. I know a healing report of an elderly gentleman who had recurring daily nightmares of war experiences and was then cured of them by his friends. The dreams tormented him for 20 years and when he was healed, he dreamt exactly the opposite: all the soldiers put their guns aside, sat down together at the laid table and talked peacefully. Sometimes bad dreams are also used by the negative side to pull us down. In this case, it is important to get rid of bad feelings and thoughts immediately in the morning and consciously open yourself up to positive things so that your soul can shine again.

But the divine side also wants to reach us through dreams and convey messages that will help us. There are numerous incidents in the Bible where God gives a person something to know through a dream in order to protect them or put them on the right path.

I myself experienced from the age of 24 that dreams are sometimes a message from God or arise from our inner divine wisdom. At that time, I had a friend who I liked very much, but who seemed emotionally cold to me. Perhaps I also overwhelmed him with the fact that I wanted affection and love from him, but he was unable to give it to me. During this time, I dreamt several times that I was in my basement room, saw my boyfriend at the window and wanted to touch him several times, but the pane of glass always separated us. I was able to decipher the dream with my psychologist. The transparent but solid pane represented the mental and emotional level that separated us. Although the mind argued: "But this must work, we've been together for so long", the clear feeling of separation ultimately won out. I realised then that there is an inner wisdom within us that knows the truth, we just have to open ourselves up to it.

An engineer I knew told me the following: When tasks at his workplace remained unsolved, he would ask for a solution in the evening before going to bed. At night, he then had the right inspirations in his dreams or the solutions were whispered into his ear. That's why he always had a pen and pad next to his bed so that he could write down the messages immediately.

An elderly lady we know once told us how tuning into the healing current / "Heilstrom" and the symbol of the butterfly had helped her when she went home and at her husband's funeral. She wished for a sign at the grave that her husband was well. And again her companions - butterflies - came, this time flying buoyantly around the gravestone. She was happy and grateful for this quick response. I was very moved by the description and thought how my father would be in the afterlife. That night I dreamt that he appeared to me, my sister and my mum in the kitchen in a bright light and he took us all in his arms one by one. That was wonderful. A sceptic might argue: "That was just a dream, insignificant, has nothing to do with reality. Dreams are foams." For me, it was a direct answer from the divine world to my question and I thanked the heavens. Once we are consciously plugged into the great divine system, we become sensitive to the signs that life itself gives us. Another example:

When my husband and I were leading a circle, I was very hurt by a criticising letter from a participant. I couldn't get any rest in the evening and couldn't fall asleep. I only fell asleep at 3.00 a.m. and when I woke up, the dream was still very vivid in my mind. I was ready to dance with someone I really valued. A dance teacher corrected our posture several times so that we could move together in complete synchronisation and harmony. I was able to interpret my dream myself: be humble, allow yourself to be corrected and have mistakes pointed out to you, this serves you and the whole. But don't let yourself be offended!

I was also able to experience that spiritually very mature people or masters have the ability to convey messages to us in dreams. When I spent the night with the then leader of the circle after a Christmas party in Sauerland with the host couple Bette, I dreamt of the leader. When we had breakfast together in the morning, she looked at me with a smile and said that she had dreamt of a cucumber salad that was now on the table. I realised immediately that she knew about my dream. She smiled when I told her about the dream in which she was one of the main protagonists. I dreamt about her a few more times later. Another time was when I had somewhat withdrawn from my voluntary work. One morning, just before I woke up, I heard her say the following words out loud: "Don't run away, keep going!" Once again, I had a dream about this matter. Four weeks before she went home, I saw her lying on her bed in a dream, close to dying. When she went home, I fell into a great sadness. I would have liked to tell her something that had remained unspoken between us. I made several heartfelt appeals to the heavenly "angelic world" to tell her certain things about me. The following night, I dreamt about her. In the dream I was at a conference that Grete Häusler was leading. I thought: "Strange, she's already dead." During the break, I went for a walk and sat down on a bench. I saw her sitting on the grass, she smiled at me and said: "Be happy." When I woke up, I was relieved. To this day, I am convinced that my message was conveyed to her and that she herself answered me in my dream. When her son took over, I dreamt that he picked my husband and me up on a raft on a raging river (the life). We were to follow his lead.

I had three dreams about neighbourly matters. I was advised by the divine world how I should behave. I asked the Lord God several times for my husband to give him help and guidance in a certain situation through a dream or an experience, which then happened. My husband had interesting dreams in which his situation was shown to him from a higher divine level. This was always an important message for him, e.g. to take his life into his own hands. In a dream, he saw himself lying in his open hand. In another dream, he was sitting by the sea and tapping the surface of the water with a long stick. Suddenly a man came up out of the water, moving towards him sadly and struggling for help. My husband ran away in fright. He then realised that this man was a reflection of his own subconscious, in which something negative was still stored that needed to be released.

For me, dreams are no longer foams. Perhaps you also wish to receive instructions and answers in your dreams. If you open yourself up inwardly, you too can experience this.

Chapter 17
On to the next quantum leap in life

Life gives us ample opportunity to learn. We are all here on earth in a great school of life. However, most people do not realise this and consider life situations to be coincidence or fate over which we have no control. But what is happening now is the effect of our thoughts and actions from the past. What we think, feel and say today has an effect on tomorrow, on our future. Everyone here on earth is guided in their own individual way. Every person on earth has their innermost being reflected back to them by the cosmos in exactly the way that is right for them. If you think about how many reflections we receive from other people in a lifetime, reflections of our own actions and how many of them we give out ourselves without realising it, it is unique. From a global perspective, this is a gigantic divine interplay with each other with the aim of moving everyone forward.

But did we know and utilise this? Probably not. We may not like some of the reflections or resonances, or we may feel unfairly treated. But God does not make mistakes. Nothing happens without us having first created the causes ourselves. The basic truth is that we are children of God. God wants us to recognise and live out the powerful and creative potential that He has placed within us. If you also want to become an awakened child of the cosmos, He will give you this experience. You can then use the life you have been given to become free of all old dross, negative programming and conditioning from the past. All blockages, all mental straitjackets, cramps and any rigidity within you can be released. This requires these reflections and resonances, which show you that there is still something that needs to be released and healed. If you then ask God for His spiritual assistance during these trials, He will help you through His love and guidance. In a situation like this, it is good to feel the closeness of helpful people who support you. The freer and more loving you become, the more the positive radiates into the cosmos and influences other people to act in the same way. In doing so, you make real quantum leaps and help others to do the same. This is why we allow forgiveness, kindness and love to prevail in interpersonal relationships when trials arise. Because everything negative can only be dissolved through tangible love.

Here are some examples of quantum leaps

17.1 Who dares, wins

That is a statement that is really true. If you want to take a risk, you need courage. I often lacked that in the past, especially in the time before I became involved with spiritual things. If I didn't like something, either professionally or in my partnership, I was annoyed and often took a long time to change the situation. Sometimes only when there was a certain amount of suffering. When you want to do something new, thoughts like: "Who knows if it will work, better stick with the old, you know what you've got." In my experience, many people simply lack the courage and confidence to try something new. They prefer to stay in their familiar situation, which at least offers them security. But they are not really happy with it.

Through my healings and the many experiences I have had over the years, I have become steadily more courageous. Because we can assume that God always wants the best for us. He wants us to be happy. And He will give us opportunities and chances through life to achieve our wishes and goals. When I kept thinking about making another career change, I simply checked my heart and gut feeling to see how I felt about the idea. As I had a good feeling, I simply started researching. In doing so, I was able to recognise how guides were already being used, which brought me to my goal very quickly and showed me which institution I should start my training with. I decided in favour of the distance learning course to become a spa and wellness trainer at the European Training Institute for Wellness and Health. I thought I had read the terms and conditions carefully, but I had overlooked the fact that this also included a written thesis (diploma) to obtain the title. With hindsight, I can say that it's a good thing I didn't read it, otherwise I wouldn't have dared. The training, which also included monthly practical attendance phases, was demanding and really good.

I was given the task of creating a slimming concept (weight reduction) for a wellness centre. I was disappointed and outraged, as I wanted a project that focussed on relaxation. I immediately contacted the institute and explained that I was very slim and not interested in the subject. The co-leader explained that the subject assignments were drawn by lot with the hope that everyone would get the right one. I was surprised at first, but I didn't really like the idea of having to deal with this unpopular subject. It worked and struggled within me until I decided to ask God to give me signs as to whether it was now my task to tackle this project.

In the evening, my husband was googling on the internet and kept seeing adverts for weight loss products. He called me and said: "You're already getting a lot of information." Yes, really, was that supposed to be a sign? I liked it, but it wasn't enough to convince me. One day later, I went into a health food shop. A saleswoman was explaining to a customer about a new weight loss product. I pricked up my ears and listened. Another clue. I made a note of the name of the product. When I wanted to go into a pharmacy afterwards, I saw a huge poster on the door with the inscription "Leichter leben in Deutschland (LLD)". By now I was already smiling at the new indication that I would probably be dealing with this topic in the next few months after all. I went to the pharmacy and read up on this weight loss method. I then wanted to buy some groceries, went into a shop and walked up to a table lined with books on this very subject. It couldn't have been made any clearer to me, three signs in one day.

I gave in and dedicated myself to this topic. I felt supported and guided, even while writing the dissertation. When heaven, life and God himself are behind us and something, it's just a great feeling. When the day of the written and oral exams came, the unpleasant thing was that the oral exam had to be taken in the morning and the written exam in the afternoon at 1.00 pm during the low performance phase. The reason for this was that the head of the institute had to leave at lunchtime. This turned out to be an advantage. I felt very confident, but I was also a little nervous and had palpitations. I placed a picture of Jesus and Bruno Gröning on my thighs and absorbed the energy while the exam papers were handed out. I had learnt enough, but I was unsure or didn't know anything about some of the questions. I asked questions to the invigilator, who acted and looked like an angel. Because the others felt disturbed, I went to her a few times. I asked her if I had ticked the right box. She didn't answer. The lady reassured me and encouraged me to take things calmly, saying: "You can do it". I actually felt calm inside and found the right solution myself. I was very touched and grateful for this.

I felt it was a divine reward to have simply dared to try something new. According to the motto: "If you go this way, then I'm all in." I got the best possible grade with guidance from the highest authority. After investing so much money and time, I thought about opening a massage studio. Will I do it? Will I not do it? Am I good enough? Does it make sense to start here in this small place? I asked God again for signs if I could venture into this endeavour. After I had massaged my twin sister, she was very enthusiastic. She gave me courage and encouraged me to just go for it.

During a Sunday walk along the Amper river in Dachau, I noticed something decorated on the stones some distance from the water. Like a magnet, I was drawn in that direction at first sight. It was a shamanic arrangement, a heart covered with moss, stones, flowers, sticks and feathers had been lovingly placed. Inside the arrangement was a note with the text: *"Every beginning is protected by a wonderful spell. Have faith."* I was really moved to tears because it fitted my situation perfectly. My husband then cycled back to the flower arrangement in the afternoon to photograph it. When he arrived at the place, he met the lady who had made it. Interestingly, the note with the inscription had not been put there by her. It had been done by an unknown person.

A few days later, I was standing in front of an esoteric shop in Dachau and looked at a text that said what the stars were telling us. It said that if you want change in your life, you should do it now. That was the third sign and I made the decision to go for it. I had the wonderful experience of seeing my studio opening on the front page of the first Christmas edition of the Dachauer Rundschau newspaper. I have now been working in my wellness oasis for 15 years and am happy to have taken the plunge. It's not as difficult as you might think. Make the decision and take the first steps, then the whole thing takes off on its own. You will experience guidance and help that you never expected. If you have a longing, a desire, a seemingly unattainable goal, dare to take the first steps! Then the signposts for the next stages will appear. Because every new beginning is protected as if by a marvellous spell. If this path doesn't turn out to be the right one, at least you will have had a completely new experience and perhaps this is an ideal springboard to the right start into happiness.

Every beginning is protected by a marvellous spell.
Have faith!

17.2 Using offence, anger and criticism to make the next quantum leap

In the course of my life, I have realised that feeling offended or criticised is a very sensitive subject for most people. Even well-intentioned advice needs to be given carefully so that the other person doesn't feel hurt.

Offences and criticism have always affected me a lot in the past. Before I became involved with spiritual things, it was particularly bad. It often took me days to recover from my "inner wounds". It took even longer before I was able to forgive this person. I learnt from Bruno Gröning's statement that offending and feeling offended makes you ill. I realised this more and more in the course of my life.

As an offended person, you feel like you've been hit with a spear, it hurts, you suffer. We cannot and should not assume and expect that all people will only say kind words to us, because none of us is perfect. And if we respond to critical words in this way, we probably already have a well-rehearsed life pattern. We attract everything that is in our thoughts and feelings and in our subconscious according to the law of attraction. But not to hurt us again, no, it comes to us because we attract it. Perhaps we have hurt people deeply ourselves in the past and this programme is now coming back to us through another person. In any case, as children of God, we should not allow ourselves to be hurt. But if it does happen, we must close the vulnerable weak spot in ourselves in order to become invulnerable. It is important not to allow ourselves to be offended and not to return what is unkind.

If you simply take an unbiased look at the comments, there may even be some good pointers on how I could improve or grow internally. In this way, the supposed troublemakers become ambassadors and teachers of our lives. In this context, Mr Robert Betz[24] talks about "arse angels"; people who may say or reflect something unpleasant to us, but on the other hand serve us like an angel. They bring up many things in us that we should dispose of. After all, we can only progress and grow inwardly by receiving advice, even if it is sometimes given to us in an unpleasant way. The following case study illustrates this:

Years ago, my husband and I took part in a mountain hiking week in Austria. On the first morning, all the participants were asked to line up in a large circle on the sports field. As I walked onto the pitch to find a space in the circle, I felt an inner insecurity inside me. As I lined up, I placed myself slightly in front of another lady, who reacted quite angrily. I was almost startled; she had hit me in my insecurity. The lady realised this without any feeling of remorse and I soon found another place to join the queue. It took me quite a while to remove the painful sting from me and let it go. That day, thoughts of the incident came back to me a few times and again I began to wonder what could have possessed this woman to react so unkindly. But I realised that this was my wounded ego coming out and that I could learn something from it. So I managed to forgive the lady because I could now look at things from a different perspective.

The next day, I stood in front of a shop window displaying scarves with a heart-shaped metal pendant. I had always wanted to own something like that. I looked at a scarf that I particularly liked. This same woman was standing on the other side of the shop. She was also looking at the display with all the heart scarves. When we both looked at each other, we couldn't help but smile. The heart as a symbol of love connected us very quickly. I went into the shop and we

---

24 The spiritual role of the "arse angels" in our lives

struck up a conversation. She consoled me that nothing had happened and smiled at me sheepishly. The lady helped me to choose the right scarf. We were both happy about this reconciliatory encounter.

But there were other tests on the subject. When we pulled into the driveway of our guesthouse one evening at 10.30 pm, one of our car's V-belts squealed loudly. The landlady's 25-year-old granddaughter ripped open the window and swore at us loudly. Then she closed the window again. My husband and I looked at each other. We felt like we were in a different film. I asked my husband if he had just heard that too. For the first few moments, we didn't know whether to laugh or be outraged. I remembered what a dear friend of mine had said: "If you get really upset about something, you still need the exam." We decided to laugh about this incident and treat it as a test, even though it was still lingering a little. In the morning, the landlady's granddaughter looked visibly embarrassed. My husband spoke to her nicely and that was the end of it.

That same day, we went for a hike. When we arrived at the mountain hut, we sat down and, hungry as I was, I unpacked the rest of my sandwiches. The mountain hut owner made a ridiculing remark about it, which all the other guests heard. I could feel the blood rising in my face and would have loved to sink into the ground. I was already embarrassed. He could have told me at the table. However, I quickly forgave the mountain hut owner, as the hut was his livelihood. But I wondered why these things happened to me so often? The next day, we had decided on a tour to Lake Gosau. We split up into the cars available for the journey.

During our car journey, I spoke to a lady about these incidents and how people were so unfriendly to me. She told me that this was a recurring theme. Grete Häusler had said at the time: "Recognise the helpful love of God behind these experiences, which shows you where you still have weaknesses and should change. Don't be offended, don't be angry about it." I felt guided and recognised through this good conversation the love of God that was sending me this information. Yes, what could or can I learn from these incidents? Definitely that I shouldn't take everything in life so seriously, but should always keep a dose of divine humour. That I should never allow myself to be offended. That I should not make my well-being dependent on the opinions and criticism of others and therefore take responsibility for my own life. That I reject false claims in a friendly but firm manner. That I should always maintain love for myself and others in everything.

Mr Gröning made a very interesting comment on the subject of "offence" in one of his lectures: *"Do I play the offended party? No, I use the split second. If someone slaps me in the face, I'm delighted. I know that he has now given up all the bad things about himself, now he is free. Then the person is like a freshly ploughed field, and I give him a good seed, a good word in his soul, which can then bear fruit. If you do this, you have really done a work of charity."*

The freer we ourselves become from all 'dross', the more we can help others. The more lightness, love and joy we have within us, the more relaxed and compassionate we become towards the negativities of other people who also need redemption. The more we come to terms with ourselves and set ourselves the goal of making the world a brighter place, the more we can act as Mr Gröning advises. This makes us happy and has a ripple effect. Bruno Gröning suggested: "These good emanations extend into the cosmos." This is exactly what the latest science assumes today, because we are connected to the universe and everything in it. It is very worthwhile to take part in this transformation process.

17.3 Making quantum leaps with humility and forgiveness

"The winner is always the one who
can love, tolerate and forgive."
Hermann Hesse

"Being humble" sounds so submissive. But it's not! It also has nothing to do with putting up with everything. It has something to do with being honest with yourself: looking at something, an incident, honestly and objectively. How did that happen? Did I also contribute to the situation getting so out of hand? Am I perhaps even the main culprit?

We already know that everything we send out comes back to us. When we are criticized by others and things are rude and mean, can we be honest with ourselves and admit that we are also a contributor to it? Ideally, yes. Then we admit our misbehaviour to ourselves and also to the other person. If we do this, then it is humility and a sign of strength of character! It shows that we take responsibility for a mistake ourselves and don't just blame others. If we then forgive the person for their misdeed and treat them with love, we have already matured into a benefactor. The other person will then be more forgiving and inclined to behave in the same way. If, on the other hand, we only blame and criticise the other person, then a conflict is inevitable, which can drag on for a long time if the fronts harden. I have observed over two decades that most people are unable to admit their own mistakes to themselves and certainly not to their neighbour. Criticism is perceived as pure humiliation; that is the worst thing for many people. It scratches at their self-esteem or makes them feel exposed. I overheard a conversation yesterday in which a gentleman spoke about this very topic. He commented that many people are inclined to dish out rebukes and criticism, but can't take it themselves and are extremely sensitive to it. Jesus also addresses this topic in his Sermon on the Mount in Matthew 7, verse 3, when he says: *"But why do you see the mote in your brother's eye and do not perceive the beam in your own eye?"* And it is indeed the case that if something bothers us so incredibly in our neighbour, where we are offended, we are certainly dealing with this issue ourselves. It wants to be resolved. The other person is just showing it to us, like a mirror that I look into. We should always start tidying up with ourselves. Then we feel happy because we have managed to get rid of it ourselves. And perhaps we recognise a need behind our neighbour's misconduct. We begin to help them and pray for them. As a result, the other person sees the example in us and also makes progress.

In the past, there was a person who always blamed others for their own discomfort. I was often her target for humiliation. Over time, this went quite deep into my soul and I lost my love for her. I prayed about this matter and clearly got the thought: "Love her." But I couldn't do that anymore at that point. I first distanced myself from this person both internally and externally. I asked myself: "Why could she hit me like that?"

On closer and more honest reflection, I realised that I also had parts of the deplorable behaviour in me and that I was still very much a human being. Then I met a spiritual woman who told me that we are all victims of victims with our negative behaviour. Can you still be angry with a victim who has had this behaviour instilled in them by their ancestors? Yes, that really made sense to me. It clicked and I was able to look at the deep humiliations from a different perspective. I also wanted to move on with myself and grow spiritually. I was able to forgive this person and sent them strength and love. This resulted in a real friendship.

In another case, I experienced humiliation and "ridicule" in the worst possible way, which really pushed me to my limits. But boundaries are there to be overcome and broken. That was very difficult for me in this case. I had suffered deep emotional and physical hurt and felt resentment and anger in my heart for these people. At the same time, however, I also recognised my part in the misconduct that had led to this entrenched situation. I spoke a lot with friends from my circle of acquaintances and they encouraged me again: "You're really bitter, give it all up, offer peace." But my inner bastard prevented me from doing so. What slowly helped me to turn things around was that I kept getting help and advice from the good side of God.

For example, in the Radio Horeb programme "Lebenshilfe" by Christa Meves on 15 March 2018, I listened to the topic:
"Streithähne" - Liebe zwischen Anmaßung und Enttäuschung: Was steckt hinter dem Streit?
"Quarrels" - Love between presumption and disappointment: What's behind the quarrel?

It was really helpful and interesting. Another time, when I was having bad thoughts again, I heard the words on the radio: "Don't hit back! Don't hit back!" It was Christian advice not to act like Cain, who killed Abel. Because I had sometimes really raised my fist to strike back mentally. Once I spontaneously opened a book and read an account of a lady's experience of how to manage to love unpleasant people. I was always very happy to see the helping signs; I realised once again that I was going through a life test. It is an opportunity to progress spiritually, to break out of old habits, to act in a new way and to experience a quantum leap in consciousness.

The symbol of the heart also became a guide and helper for me throughout this time. Never before in my life have I encountered so many hearts in any form as during this difficult time of testing. Often fitting when I was once again thinking about this matter. A heart in the butter I spread on bread, a heart formed when I poured water on a flannel. Hearts in the shape of stones, leaves, a potato heart, a purple heart on a tree trunk, a large heart as a car advert, to name but a few. They all called me to stay in the heart frequency, to love, to forgive and to be humble.

I also dreamt several times at night about the people with whom I now saw myself on good terms in my dreams. Nevertheless, my inner bastard tormented me and I found it very difficult to put things into practice. I had often been annoyed by these people. But they behaved as if they wanted to tell me: "What do you want, we're just behaving so that you can learn something." I would have liked them to change their behaviour, but I received three hints that I should change my inner attitude.

A few times I asked God and his helpers whether I shouldn't leave the situation. I was told that I was in the exact place where I could learn a lot, that I shouldn't be so sensitive. I was standing in my own way when it came to doing the right thing. Yes, I was even told not to be so sensitive. I thought: "Is this information coming from the divine source, that I shouldn't behave like this?" It was! Life sometimes challenges us quite a lot, but that's part of real life.

Pastor Peter Maier also spoke on this topic in his eighth retreat speech on Radio Horeb. He compared people to a rough diamond that is polished through life. We should allow this process in order to grow inwardly, to learn to remain in love in all situations, because the word of God is something living that would also endure and work in all storms of life. The words shook me up and I renewed my desire to make it. I asked God for his help. During a hiking holiday in Austria, a spiritual local approached me. We didn't know each other and yet he said something to me that fitted my situation perfectly: "Girl, you're in a difficult situation, you'll make it, you'll make it in love!" After a while, I managed it and I was able to be forgiving and loving towards people again. I realised that I had made a quantum leap as a result.

I am describing this situation in more detail because it is precisely these issues in the interpersonal sphere that are always topical and can push us to our limits. But love knows no boundaries, it wants to work through us everywhere. After this time, a saying came to mind that I liked so much when I read it: "The way back to oneself is a heroic deed ..." This is the path back to the true self, to becoming a child of God, which bubbles over with positive emotions and clears away and overcomes all negativity. Then we come into our true element and feel at ease.

17.4 Making quantum leaps with love and compassion

"Love is the strongest power in the world, and yet it is
the humblest imaginable."
Mahatma Gandhi

Love and compassion are balm for the soul. When a person treats us with loving words and compassionate gestures, it feels good. We can enjoy it, but we shouldn't be dependent on other people's love or recognition. I was for a long time in my life and it didn't make me happy. It is better to have so much love in our hearts that we can give it to others. Then we experience the truth of Jesus' statement: *"It is more blessed to give than to receive"*. Because the gratitude, love and joy of the recipient returns to our heart many times over. But we should also be careful when giving. If we focus too much on others, we neglect ourselves. Everyone should listen to how their body feels and assess for themselves how much energy and time they can invest in loving their neighbour. God is love. Therefore, we are all children of love. If we allow God to give us this awareness and this love at the source, we are on the right path. It is very important that we pay enough attention to ourselves and treat ourselves with love. We often have so many things in our heads that need to be done, overdraw our energy account or lose ourselves in ambition for material things and goals. We then feel this physically.

Years ago, a spiritual lady who sometimes advises me on health matters said to me: "You don't treat yourself with enough love." I was surprised at first. I didn't even realise it, but it was true. I still tended to do more than my energy levels allowed: too little holiday and recovery periods during exams. I then made some changes in the right direction and gave myself more attention, time and, above all, love again. My body thanked me for it.

For example, you can not only take in oxygen with your breath, but also consciously absorb a lot of healing energy. Or use your attention to send loving thoughts and feelings to individual organs, joints and bones that may not yet be completely healthy. It can help if you lay your hands on them. Because every organ, even every cell, is its own individual, which has a divine inner control and needs care. Consolation, thanksgiving and love are gratefully accepted by the cells. It is like a blessing. The loving radiations of our self reach into the atoms and help to restore order. I like a statement by Bruno Gröning very much and it fits here: *"Man is a creature of love. And what is created in love can only live in love."* How many radiations from wrong thoughts, feelings and experiences we often have to cope with and have let the bad things into our souls. We can feel this very quickly in our cells and body. This is why it is very important to clear out our minds, absorb energy through the healing current / "Heilstrom" and love our bodies. Even the Swiss physician Paracelsus said in the 16th century that the highest form of medicine is love. It should therefore not be missing from any treatment or application.

Everything we think, talk and express emotionally about someone is received and helps or harms them. We have to be aware of that. This is exactly what I have realised more and more clearly on this spiritual path. There is no point in condemning someone for an offence. We are all called upon to forgive them and to set an example with our own lives. Over the decades, when I have been able to show love and compassion to others, I have seen all my problems dissolve. A few times in my life, I or someone close to me have been so offended or treated so cruelly that I thought: "I can never forgive that again and I certainly can't love that person any more."

But I could feel in my body that this behaviour was making me ill and acting as a blockage on my own path in life. As a result, we burden the other person with guilt. There are plenty of cases where an argument or a disturbance between people has not been resolved for a lifetime. Even death does not dissolve this negative entanglement. Only forgiveness, love and understanding can restore harmony. It often helps to empathise with the other person's situation and look at things from their point of view. Why is the other person acting this way?

At the time, Mr Gröning replied to the people who criticised him: "You don't know why he is acting like this." Just look at all the chaotic warfare in this world. We don't know how many cruelties and injustices have been inflicted on people, who then react with brute force or become murderers. All atrocities are always the bitter consequence of suffering unkindness, despair and a lack of understanding. This is why Jesus said 2,000 years ago: *"Love your enemies and do good to those who hate you."* (Luke 6:27)

Buddha expresses this with the following words: *"Never in the world does hate end through hate, hate ends through love."* Only those who look with the heart and allow compassion and love to prevail will release the sting in the other person.

If you cannot get out of judging other people, the wheel of fate will turn at some point in your life and the "judgeer" will find himself in such a situation where he is judged and longs for understanding. This helps them to see the situation from the other person's point of view and to become more insightful and forgiving. I have experienced this myself several times and have also been able to observe it in other fates. Even the prophet Mohammed said in this context: *"He who is not merciful will not find mercy."* In Luke, chapter 6, verse 38, Jesus warns *"... for with the same measure that you use, you will be measured again."* We should always treat our fellow human beings as we would like to be treated ourselves. If we are generous and forgiving, it will often come back to us.

Life is about developing more and more love and compassion for yourself and your fellow human beings. Especially for people who are socially marginalised, people of a different skin colour and religion, for people who are unfriendly, argumentative and so very different from us. I read an appropriate saying in a local office: *"Unfriendly people need a lot of kindness."* And so it is!

Let's do as Bruno Gröning did, who let people who scolded or slapped him leave until they had given up everything that was bad. Then he responded with good words and thoughts and extinguished the negative flame. The more love we carry within us and radiate, the brighter and lighter the world becomes.

Chapter 18
All global problems can be solved
in a new consciousness

The fact that we are connected to everything on earth and in the cosmos via an energy field and that our thoughts and feelings can have an effect on matter gives us the opportunity to have a positive and healing effect on the problems of our time.

Climate change with its negative consequences, global warming, the melting of the poles, environmental pollution, acid rain, to name just a few effects of the wrong actions and thoughts of people on earth. How can these effects be brought to a halt and how can things be put back in order? Is it enough just to reduce or stop CO_2 emissions or to take other external measures?

In my opinion, that is not enough. The earth is something holistically alive that also suffers if it is treated unlovingly. And the approximately 8 billion inhabitants of the earth, who often only revolve around their problems and thus become spiritual polluters, do it no good either. As I was writing this chapter, I listened to Father Robert Maria's sermon on Radio Horeb at 9.00 a.m. on 25 Oct. 2019. He was of the same opinion that it is not enough just to reduce pollutants to preserve the earth, but that the problem is much deeper. The earth and all of creation are feeling the effects of humanity's wrong thinking, speaking and acting. It is crying out to be redeemed. He was referring to St Paul's letter to the Romans.

Romans 8, verses 21-22 *says: "For the whole creation will be set free from the bondage of corruption into the glorious liberty of the children of God. For we know that the whole of creation has been groaning and anguishing with us up to this moment."*

A turnaround in thought and action is necessary so that creation can also be redeemed through the redemption of humanity. Each of us can send tangible love to the earth, for example by embrace it lovingly in our imagination. These beneficial radiations reach her, she is strengthened and built up. The feeling of love is the highest vibration in the cosmos and it also has an effect on the atoms of the elements such as the earth. Anyone who is filled with the sanctifying power that comes from God can pass this mission on to humanity and the whole earth.

Many members of the global circle, including myself, do this every day. We use the creation potential of our hearts and ask for clean water and clean air, for the normalisation of the climate, for the right pH value of the water or for the poles to form more ice again. Anything is possible if many people ask and believe in a living way. The more people do this, the greater the effect. The more regenerative power the earth has, the sooner the balance can be restored. The author Neville comes to the following realisation in his book "The Power of Awareness":

"The power of our conviction is a force against which no earthly force has even the slightest significance."

That is a very strong statement, which my husband as a physicist and I can only emphasise. The power of our conviction and faith overcomes even known physical laws or even overrides them, as can be seen, for example, in an undamaged firewalk over glowing coals. Just as tumours can disappear in a human body through the power of prayer and firm faith, or bones can be replenished in the case of osteoporosis, so deep faith in the heart and the transmission of power can initiate regeneration processes here on earth that are astonishing. For example, my husband told me that the sun has been shining very calmly for a long time and no longer has any strong ejections. As a result, it doesn't burn so strongly and protects the poles. Or that seas that have been polluted with a lot of oil have developed strains of bacteria that eat up the oil. The whole of nature is something divine, an entire ecological system that has always been designed to be self-sustaining.

However, human abuse must not be allowed to go any further so that the entire ecosystem does not collapse at some point. A holistic and global rethink and action is required in future from every individual, from companies, corporations, governments and world powers that have the overall well-being of humanity and the preservation of our creation as their main focus.

If people grow back into this sense of responsibility for themselves and creation and experience who they are and what their hearts are capable of, all environmental problems can be solved. That is my firm conviction after all the experiences I have had. The power and authority to love from our hearts, to ask, to let visions and wishes become reality through our faith, to be able to fill up on divine healing currents from the cosmos, which carry a great potential for healing and creation, allow me to look to the future with confidence.

In these times of upheaval, everything can and should be healed again and regulated for the better. This starts here on earth with us humans. The desire for healing, for peace and the willingness to be transformed into a higher consciousness is growing more and more. To achieve this, all negative characteristics and areas are brought to the surface and uncovered. This can be a painful process, which then initiates this path for us. That is why we all need a lot of compassion, understanding and love for ourselves and for our fellow human beings in order to move forward together in this healing process. If this happens, then the earth and the whole of creation can also be healed.

The World Peace Prayer Society also appreciated this and presented the current head of the circle, Dieter Häusler, with the Peace Pole Award in May 2013 at the UN Corporate Chapel in New York as a very special honour for his valuable and selfless work. UN representative Deborah Moldow said the following words, among others, at the presentation of the Peace Pole Award:

"When our body is whole, we call it health
and when our world is whole, we call it peace.
And by healing ourselves, we heal the world."

Let's look forward to the future and let's all help in this great transformation process into a new special time.

Your heart moves the world

Epilogue

It was my heartfelt desire to emphasise how connected each and every one of us is to the whole of creation. How much our thoughts, feelings and beliefs influence not only our body in a positive or negative way, but also our environment and the whole of creation.

It is impressive that each of us has been given so much power, but it also brings with it the responsibility to use it in the right way. with it. Check your beliefs. Are they still true after reading this book?

I am delighted if I have been able to give you, dear reader, some inspiration to embark on a new adventure in life. Because we can start afresh every day, no matter where we are in life at the moment. Perhaps you feel the courage to want to leave something old to start something new: a different flat, a better job, the right partner, whatever it is. If you have the desire in your heart, go for it! Don't listen to your doubting mind, because life itself will help you.

Perhaps you are beginning to harbour the hope that it is still possible to get well after all. Then take this path to health. Find a path, a doctor, a group that will help you. When you take the first steps, you will already be guided. If you want to absorb the divine healing powers from the cosmos yourself, you can learn this in the circle, where you will also learn the rules of life that Mr Gröning knew. Or you can search for another group on the Internet or suddenly find out from a colleague at work, for example, that there is something there. Because if you search, you will find it. Do you suddenly have the feeling that you need to clean out yourself and your cupboards? Start with that! Get things moving, maybe things will change without you actively doing anything. Would you like to be able to live more from the heart again, to feel love? Then talk to the Lord God and ask Him for all these things. He will be able to give them to you. He will find a way to reach you if you are serious about it. Then you can speak to everything in creation with your awakened heart, try it out. It is interesting to observe what can then happen. Then you will experience that your heart can move the world. One thing is certain, that you have God's blessing with every new beginning and that He loves you eternally and infinitely.

I wish you all the best on your personal path to happiness.

December 2024

Acknowledgement

I thank the almighty heavenly Father from the bottom of my heart that He has shown me how much He loves me and that His love endures through all my shortcomings and mistakes. I bow before His foresighted, profound wisdom, His omnipotence and power, which always want to guide everything for the best. I consider the many helpings, healings and realisations I have experienced as special gifts and as a divine treasure that will remain with me forever.

I would like to thank Bruno Gröning, who, through his great mission, his life and his suffering, made the teachings of Christ understandable and tangible for me. I would also like to thank Grete Häusler for her tireless efforts in showing me and over 80,000 people worldwide the path to salvation. Through her example, I was able to learn so much and apply it to my life in a beneficial way.

I also feel very close to the couple Thea and Werner Bette, who helped me on this spiritual path for the first six years. I thank the Circle of Friends under the leadership of Dieter Häusler and his wife Birgit for their guidance and help. I honour Gregg Braden for his lecture "In tune with the divine matrix", which confirmed all my insights.

I also pay tribute to my "teachers" and "tormentors", because they helped me to recognise where I had and still have room for improvement.

I am deeply grateful to my dear husband and soul mate for being so helpful, diligent and creative at my side during the layout and design of this book. I send a loving hug to Julia Oppermann, who edited this book, and to my sister Birgit, who was a good counsellor in all matters. I would like to thank all the helpers who, guided by God, gave me important advice.

Your heart moves the world